AIR FRYER

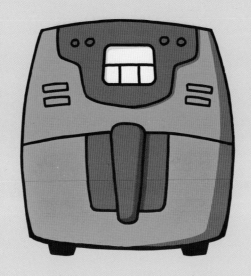

Quarto.com

© 2025 Quarto Publishing Group USA Inc.
Text © 2021 Michelle Anderson
Photography © 2020 Leigh Olson, except those noted below

First Published in 2025 by The Harvard Common Press, an imprint of The Quarto Group,
100 Cummings Center, Suite 265-D, Beverly, MA 01915, USA.
T (978) 282-9590 F (978) 283-2742

The Harvard Common Press titles are also available at discount for retail, wholesale, promotional, and bulk purchase. For details, contact the Special Sales Manager by email at specialsales@quarto.com or by mail at The Quarto Group, Attn: Special Sales Manager, 100 Cummings Center, Suite 265-D, Beverly, MA 01915, USA.

29 28 27 26 25   1 2 3 4 5

ISBN: 978-0-7603-9743-5

Digital edition published in 2025
eISBN: 978-0-7603-9744-2

Library of Congress Cataloging-in-Publication Data

Names: Harvard Common Press, editor.
Title: Air fryer / editors of the Harvard Common Press.
Description: Beverly, MA, USA : Harvard Common Press, 2025. | Series: The
   time pressed cook | Includes bibliographical references and index.
Identifiers: LCCN 2024054043 | ISBN 9780760397435 (hardcover) | ISBN
   9780760397442 (ebook)
Subjects: LCSH: Hot air frying.
Classification: LCC TX689 .A483 2025 | DDC 641.7/7--dc23/eng/20241205
LC record available at https://lccn.loc.gov/2024054043

The content in this book was previously published in *Epic Air Fryer Cookbook* by Emily Paster (Harvard Common Press, 2019) and *Epic Air Fryer Plant-Powered Cookbook* by Michelle Anderson (Harvard Common Press, 2021).

Design and Page Layout: Megan Jones Design
Photography: Leigh Olson on pages 7, 10, 13, 18, 22, 26, 34, 41, 43, 44, 66, 69, 75, 79, 83, 84, 87, 88, 91, 92, 95, 96, 99, 100, 103, 108, 111, 113, 114, 118, and 121; Glenn Scott on pages 14, 17, 21, 25, 29, 30, 33, 37, 38, 46, 49, 53, 54, 57, 58, 61, 62, 65, 70, 73, 76, 80, 104, 107, and 117; Shutterstock on page 50
Illustration: Michael Korfhage

Printed in China

AIR FRYER

EDITORS OF THE HARVARD COMMON PRESS

HARVARD
COMMON
PRESS

CONTENTS

1
BREAKFAST AND BRUNCH
11

2
APPETIZERS, SNACKS, AND PARTY FOOD
27

3
SOUPS, SANDWICHES, SALADS, AND LUNCHES
47

INTRODUCTION: AIR FRYER BASICS

WHAT IS AN AIR FRYER? HOW DOES IT WORK?

At its heart, an air fryer is a powerful countertop convection oven. Many of us are familiar with convection ovens. The large oven in your kitchen may well have a convection feature that you use or, more likely, don't use. Convection ovens have fans and exhaust systems that move the hot air of the oven around the food being baked so that it cooks more quickly and evenly. A convection oven is also drier than a regular oven because the exhaust system whisks away any moisture that has built up in the closed oven, causing foods to become more browned and caramelized.

An air fryer is essentially a small convection oven that gets hotter and moves air faster than other convection ovens. As a result, the air fryer cooks food quickly and does an excellent job of making the exterior dry, browned, and crispy while keeping the interior moist and juicy. When you coat food with a dry breading or wrap it in pastry, and brush or spray the exterior with oil, the powerful fan circulates the tiny droplets of oil around the food, which mimics, in some ways, the effects of deep-frying.

So the air fryer can mimic the effects of deep-frying, with a small amount of oil. It can also bake and roast certain foods more evenly and in less time than it would take in an oven. What's more, the air fryer whisks away moisture, just like the convection setting on your oven, which allows it essentially to dry out foods with a lot of moisture in them, such as certain vegetables, and make them crispy and caramelized as opposed to soggy. And speaking of soggy, you know how some foods, like pizza, get limp and rubbery when you reheat them in the microwave? The air fryer solves that problem. It actually makes foods crispier upon reheating by whisking away any moisture that has accumulated from storage in the refrigerator.

To sum up, let's review what you can do with your air fryer. First, you can mimic the taste and texture of deep-fried foods—not perfectly, but pretty well—using just teaspoons and tablespoons of oil as opposed to cups. You can also bake and roast meat, fish, and vegetables—again with very little added fat—in less time and sometimes with better results than in the oven. You can reheat foods without making them limp and soggy like a microwave does. And you can do all of this without heating up the whole house and with a portable appliance that can be moved around and brought to rental and vacation homes.

Now that you know what an air fryer is and how it works, let's learn a little more about how to use your air fryer.

TIPS ON USING YOUR AIR FRYER

When using your air fryer, there are a few general principles to follow to ensure that you get deliciously consistent results:

Don't Overfill the Basket.

As mentioned before, the air fryer fan blows hot air around the food in the basket, which causes browning and caramelization. Therefore, it is important not to crowd the basket with too much food, which would prevent the air from circulating—even if that means having to cook food in two or sometimes three batches. If you overfill the basket, the food will steam instead of baking or roasting. Steamed food is limp and soggy, not brown and crispy. It is also important not to cover or line the air fryer basket with foil or parchment paper—unless the parchment paper also has holes or perforations—except in very rare instances. Also, be sure to flip or turn the food during cooking to make sure that all sides are exposed to the hot air. (The recipes usually indicate how often and when to turn food.)

Stick with Dry Batter, Not Wet.

When you think about fried foods, you may imagine foods coated with a wet batter such as tempura or a beer batter. These wet batters work well when deep-frying but not in the air fryer. The powerful fan could easily blow the batter off the food and create quite a mess inside your machine. In general, stick with a dry coating, such as flour, cornstarch, or breadcrumbs. Many of the "fried" recipes in this book call for you to coat food in flour, then dip it in an egg wash, and then, finally, coat it with dry breadcrumbs, especially Japanese panko breadcrumbs, which are exceptionally light and crispy. Following this three-part process, which you will notice throughout the book, will help the coating stick to your food and make the food's exterior as crunchy and crispy as if it were deep-fried.

Use a Little Bit of Oil (But Not EVOO).

You may have hoped to make fried foods with no oil at all in the air fryer. But you will not end up with deliciously browned and crisp foods without at least some added fat. Also, spraying the basket of the air fryer with oil prevents certain foods from sticking. For foods that you have coated with flour, breadcrumbs, or other dry coatings, spray them with oil right before cooking them in the air fryer. For foods like potatoes, vegetables, and lean meats, such as chicken without skin, brush or toss them with a little bit of oil—anywhere from a few teaspoons to a tablespoon—right before cooking. (In other words, do not oil foods in advance.) For foods that are naturally fatty, such as red meat or skin-on chicken, there is no need to add additional oil. Although extra-virgin olive oil is good for sautéing foods on the stove and for making salad dressing, it is not recommended for cooking foods in the air fryer except where specified. Extra-virgin olive oil has a low smoke point, and the air fryer cooks foods at high temperatures. Instead use a neutral-tasting oil with a high smoke point such as vegetable, canola, or grapeseed. (Where the recipes ask for vegetable oil, feel free to substitute canola or grapeseed.)

Preheat. Don't Overcook.

When using your large oven, it is absolutely essential that you let it come up to temperature before putting food in it. And that can sometimes take ten or even twenty minutes. When using your air fryer, it is helpful if you preheat it before using, but just a few minutes of preheating are necessary. And sometimes it doesn't even need that. When a dish may come out significantly better if you preheat the air fryer first, it is indicated in the recipe. On a related note, the air fryer cooks food very quickly, and remember that the fan dries food out. Be sure to watch your food carefully to prevent burning and overcooking, which could make your food dry and tough. Do not hesitate to open the drawer to check on food while it cooks, especially when you are first using your air fryer and learning how it works.

ACCESSORIES

Don't you hate it when you buy an expensive new kitchen appliance only to discover that you now have to buy a bunch of accessories to use it? The good news is that the only accessory you really must purchase to get the most out of your air fryer is an oil sprayer or mister. As explained previously, spraying breaded foods with oil is essential to achieving a crispy, crunchy, deep-fried texture, and using store-bought cooking sprays with propellants and other chemicals can damage the nonstick coating of the air fryer basket. The solution to this dilemma is to buy a refillable oil sprayer or mister that will allow you to spray your food with oil and nothing else. Purchase one specifically designed to spray oil because oil can clog the nozzle of a regular spray bottle. (In the interest of full disclosure, even the sprayers designed for oil have a tendency to clog and stop working as well after a while because oil is so viscous.)

Beyond the oil mister, there are a few additional accessories that you may want to invest in. A small cake or pizza pan that fits inside your air fryer will be helpful to make some of the breakfast and dessert recipes in this book. And because regular skewers are too long to fit in most air fryers, you may also want a set of metal skewers specially designed for your machine. There are many air fryer accessory kits on the market that have pans, skewers, and more for a reasonable price. One last kitchen accessory that is recommended for everyone is a reliable, instant-read thermometer to make sure that you are cooking meat, fish, and chicken to a safe internal temperature.

1

BREAKFAST AND BRUNCH

STRAWBERRIES AND CREAM BAKED OATMEAL

SERVES: 2 to 4

Baked oatmeal is another warm, comforting breakfast that cooks up quickly and with very little preparation using the air fryer. With whole grains from the rolled oats and protein from the milk and egg, this baked oatmeal will keep everyone in your family full and satisfied until lunch. And the berries and brown sugar make all that healthy goodness go down easily. The splash of cream makes this version of baked oatmeal taste especially rich, but if you don't have cream on hand, using all milk is fine.

Any fresh berry will work in place of the strawberries. In the summer months, try using sliced stone fruits, such as peaches and nectarines, for a seasonal treat.

1 cup (170 g) sliced strawberries

1 egg

¾ cup (180 ml) milk

¼ cup (60 ml) heavy cream

1 cup (80 g) rolled oats

2 tablespoons (19 g) brown sugar

½ teaspoon baking powder

½ teaspoon cinnamon

½ teaspoon ginger

Pinch salt

1 tablespoon (14 g) unsalted butter (optional)

....

1. Place the sliced strawberries in the bottom of the cake pan insert for the air fryer, reserving a few for garnish. In a small bowl, whisk together the egg, milk, and cream and pour it over the strawberries in the pan.

2. In a small bowl, combine the rolled oats, brown sugar, baking powder, spices, and salt. Add the dry ingredients to the wet ingredients in the cake pan and stir to combine. Allow to rest for 10 minutes. Place the reserved strawberries on top of the oatmeal.

3. Place the cake pan in the air fryer and bake at 320°F (160°C) for 15 minutes until the oatmeal is warmed through and puffed. Spoon the oatmeal into bowls. If desired, add a pat of butter to each bowl for extra richness.

1 cup (156 g) rolled oats

¼ cup (28 g) chopped pecans

¼ cup (28 g) slivered almonds

2 tablespoons (18 g) sunflower seeds

2 tablespoons (18 g) pumpkin seeds

1 tablespoon (11 g) chia seeds

⅛ teaspoon ground cinnamon

Pinch sea salt

2 tablespoons (40 g) maple syrup

1 tablespoon (15 ml) canola oil

1 ruby red grapefruit, halved crosswise

2 tablespoons (30 g) brown sugar

¼ cup (60 g) vanilla Greek yogurt

GRAPEFRUIT GRANOLA BRÛLÉE WITH GREEK YOGURT

SERVES: 2

This combination of sweet and tart is intoxicating, and the color spectacular. Topping this pretty fruit with a layer of caramelized sugar and air fryer toasty granola is an absolute treat, and you will wonder why you never tried it before.

1. Preheat the air fryer on Roast at 260°F (130°C) for 3 minutes.

2. Combine the oats, pecans, almonds, sunflower seeds, pumpkin seeds, chia seeds, cinnamon, and salt in a medium bowl. Add the maple syrup and oil and toss to coat.

3. Place the oat mixture in a 7-inch (18 cm) round baking pan and cook for 25 to 28 minutes, stirring every 7 minutes, until browned and crunchy. Spread the hot granola onto a parchment paper–lined baking sheet and let it cool to room temperature, about 45 minutes, stirring occasionally.

4. While the granola is cooling, place the grapefruit halves cut-side down on paper towels to soak up excess juice for at least 30 minutes.

5. Turn the halves cut-side up and use a paring knife to loosen the sections from the membranes, then sprinkle half the sugar on each half, spreading it out evenly. Use a kitchen torch to caramelize and melt the sugar (brûlée).

6. Top each half with ¼ to ⅓ cup (25 to 30 g) of granola and a dollop of yogurt.

7. Store the remaining granola in an airtight container for up to a week at room temperature.

FRENCH TOAST STICKS WITH CINNAMON MASCARPONE SAUCE

SERVES: 2

The trick to getting the best results in this recipe is to make sure you shake off the excess soaking mixture or the bread will be uneven in color and vaguely eggy. Add a little orange zest for a lovely citrus variation.

....

1. In a medium bowl, whisk together the milk, eggs, brown sugar, vanilla, and salt until very well blended.

2. Preheat the air fryer at 375°F (190°C) for 3 minutes. Lightly oil a 7-inch (18 cm) round baking pan.

3. Add half the bread sticks to the egg mixture, turning to coat.

4. Shake the excess egg mixture off the sticks and place them in a single layer in the pan. Spray lightly with oil and cook the sticks for 4 minutes. Turn them, spray lightly with oil, and cook for 2 to 3 minutes, or until golden brown.

5. Transfer the French toast sticks to a plate, loosely tent with foil to keep them warm, and repeat with the remaining bread sticks.

6. In a medium bowl, whisk the mascarpone, maple syrup, vanilla, cinnamon, and cloves until well mixed. Spoon the sauce into 2 small bowls and serve with warm French toast sticks.

7. Refrigerate leftover sauce in a covered container for up to 5 days.

FRENCH TOAST STICKS

½ cup (120 ml) whole milk

2 large eggs

1 tablespoon (15 g) brown sugar

1 teaspoon vanilla extract

Pinch sea salt

4 thick slices bread (such as brioche, Texas toast, French bread), cut into thirds

Oil spray

CINNAMON MASCARPONE SAUCE

1 cup (240 g) mascarpone, at room temperature

¼ cup (80 g) maple syrup

1 teaspoon vanilla extract

½ teaspoon ground cinnamon

Pinch ground cloves

FRITTERS

2 firm apples, such as Granny Smith, peeled, cored, and diced

Juice from 1 lemon

½ teaspoon cinnamon

1 cup (125 g) all-purpose flour

1½ teaspoons baking powder

½ teaspoon kosher salt

2 tablespoons (26 g) granulated sugar

2 eggs

¼ cup (60 ml) milk

2 tablespoons (28 g) unsalted butter, melted

Vegetable oil for spraying

GLAZE

1¼ cups (125 g) powdered sugar, sifted

½ teaspoon vanilla extract

¼ cup (60 ml) water

APPLE FRITTERS

MAKES: 15 fritters, to serve 4 or 5

These apple fritters are an old-fashioned sweet breakfast treat that feels as indulgent as a doughnut but without all the fat. Diced apples are folded into a cake-like batter, which is then scooped directly onto the basket of the air fryer and cooked in less than 10 minutes. Once the fritters have cooled a bit, you can give them a light glaze or simply dust with powdered sugar.

The batter tends to stick to the basket of the air fryer, so be sure to oil it well or line the basket with perforated parchment paper. Use a thin spatula that is safe for nonstick coating to remove the fritters from the basket.

....

1. To make the fritters, toss the diced apples with the lemon juice and cinnamon in a small bowl and set aside. In a large bowl, whisk together the flour, baking powder, and salt. In a medium bowl, whisk together the sugar and eggs until the mixture is pale yellow. Whisk in the milk followed by the melted butter. Add the wet ingredients to the dry ingredients in the large bowl and stir to combine. Fold in the diced apples.

2. Brush the basket of the air fryer with oil or line with perforated parchment paper to prevent sticking. Working in 3 batches and using a spring-loaded cookie scoop, ice cream scoop, or ¼-cup measure, scoop 5 balls of dough directly onto the air fryer basket. Spray the fritters with oil. Cook at 360°F (182°C) for 7 to 8 minutes until the outside is browned and the inside is fully cooked. Remove the cooked fritters to a cooling rack and repeat 2 more times with the remaining dough.

3. Make the glaze by whisking together the powdered sugar, vanilla, and water in a small bowl. (The glaze should be thin.) Drizzle the glaze over the fritters or dip the tops of the fritters directly in the glaze, letting any excess drip off.

CRISPY LATKES WITH SOUR CREAM AND APPLE

SERVES: 4

Latkes—a traditional Jewish dish—are potato pancakes made from shredded potato, onion, and garlic fried into a crispy, golden lattice, the ideal base for tender butter-sautéed apples. The air fryer creates the same texture and lovely color with very little oil and less time, but they still are very hot coming out, so don't scorch your fingers!

....

1. Place the grated potato and onion in the center of a clean kitchen cloth, fold up the sides to form a pouch, and twist, holding the ends of the pouch, to squeeze out as much liquid as possible.

2. Place the dry potato and onion in a large bowl and stir in the breadcrumbs, cornstarch, egg, and garlic powder until very well mixed. Season with salt and pepper and let the mixture stand for 10 minutes.

3. Preheat the air fryer at 360°F (182°C) for 3 minutes.

4. Spray the air fryer basket with oil. Working in batches, scoop out ¼-cup (30 g) measures of the potato mixture and form them into 3-inch (7 cm) patties. Place them in the basket in a single layer, about 4 per batch, and cook for 8 to 10 minutes, turning halfway through, until golden and crispy.

5. Transfer the cooked latkes to a plate and repeat with the remaining potato mixture.

6. While you are cooking the last batch, melt the butter in a small skillet over medium-high heat. Sauté the apples and cinnamon until tender and lightly browned, about 5 minutes. Set aside.

7. Serve the latkes warm with the apple and a dollop of sour cream. (Make sure you check the nutrition label on the sour cream—some brands contain rennet or gelatin, which are animal products.)

3 large russet potatoes, scrubbed and grated

½ small sweet onion, grated

2 tablespoons (14 g) breadcrumbs

1 tablespoon (8 g) cornstarch

1 large egg

¼ teaspoon garlic powder

Sea salt

Freshly ground black pepper

Oil spray

1 tablespoon (14 g) butter

2 apples, peeled and thinly sliced

⅛ teaspoon ground cinnamon

½ cup (115 g) sour cream

2 sweet potatoes, peeled
and cut into a small dice

1 tablespoon (15 ml)
vegetable oil (optional)

Kosher salt and pepper
to taste

6 large flour tortillas

1 can (16 ounces, or 455 g)
refried black beans, divided

1½ cups (45 g) baby spinach,
lightly packed, divided

6 eggs, scrambled

¾ cup (90 g) grated
Cheddar or Monterey Jack
cheese, divided

Vegetable oil for heating

Salsa, guacamole,
and sour cream

FREEZE-AND-FRY SWEET POTATO AND BLACK BEAN BREAKFAST BURRITOS

MAKES: 6 burritos

Breakfast burritos are a grab-and-go weekday-morning favorite. The frozen store-bought versions can be expensive and full of unfamiliar ingredients. Save money and eat healthier by making a batch of these easy breakfast burritos over the weekend and freezing them. When you wake up in the morning, pop one of the burritos into the air fryer to heat while you get ready. They only need 20 minutes to go from freezer to warm, cheesy, and ready to eat. For a crispy outside, like a chimichanga, brush the burrito with oil and heat for an additional 5 minutes.

With refried black beans, roasted sweet potatoes, spinach, scrambled eggs, and just a sprinkle of cheese, these breakfast burritos will satisfy even the hungriest appetite until lunchtime.

1. Toss the sweet potatoes with the (optional) vegetable oil and season with salt and pepper. Cook in the air fryer at 400°F (200°C) until cooked through, about 10 minutes. Remove and set aside.

2. Take a flour tortilla and spread ¼ cup (59.5 g) of the refried beans down the center, leaving a border at each end. Top with ¼ cup (8 g) of the spinach leaves. Sprinkle ¼ cup (27.5 g) plus 2 tablespoons (14 g) of sweet potato cubes on top of the spinach. Top with one-sixth of the scrambled eggs and 2 tablespoons (10 g) grated cheese. To wrap the burrito, fold the long side over the ingredients, then fold in the short sides and roll. Repeat with the remaining ingredients and tortillas.

3. Wrap each burrito tightly in foil and combine in a large, gallon-size freezer bag. Freeze for up to 3 months.

4. To heat, place the burrito, still wrapped in foil, in the air fryer and cook at 350°F (180°C) for 20 minutes, flipping once halfway through. Remove the burrito from the foil, brush the outside of the tortilla with 1 teaspoon oil, and heat for an additional 3 to 5 minutes, turning once. Serve with salsa, Roasted Garlic Guacamole (page 40), or sour cream as desired.

ROMAINE AND FETA FRITTATA

SERVES: 4

Cooked lettuce? Yes, robust lettuce like romaine, escarole, and endive are fabulous grilled, roasted, sautéed, or cooked into a creamy frittata with heaps of herbs and salty feta cheese. The taste of romaine becomes deeper and more complex, and the texture remains a little crisp. Sour cream adds an intriguing tanginess and creates a pleasing creaminess. A frittata is essentially a baked omelet, with the other ingredients baked right into the egg rather than the cooked egg folded over it. Making this frittata in an air fryer cuts the cooking time, so this tasty dish can become a regular meal even on a busy weekday.

....

1. Grease a 7-inch (18 cm) round baking pan with olive oil.

2. Melt the butter in a large skillet over medium-high heat and sauté the lettuce and onion until softened, 5 to 6 minutes. Transfer the greens to the baking pan.

3. In a medium bowl, whisk the eggs, milk, sour cream, and herbs and season with salt and pepper. Pour the eggs over the greens, stirring slightly to distribute them throughout the eggs. Top with the feta cheese.

4. Preheat the air fryer at 350°F (180°C) for 3 minutes.

5. Cook the frittata until the eggs are cooked through and light brown, about 15 minutes. Serve.

Olive oil, for greasing

2 tablespoons (28 g) butter

2 cups (110 g) shredded romaine lettuce or Swiss chard

½ small sweet onion, chopped

6 large eggs

¼ cup (60 ml) whole milk

¼ cup (60 g) sour cream

2 tablespoons (5 g) chopped mixed fresh herbs (such as basil, thyme, or oregano)

Sea salt

Freshly ground black pepper

½ cup (75 g) crumbled feta cheese

2

APPETIZERS, SNACKS, AND PARTY FOOD

SPICY ROASTED CHICKPEAS

SERVES: 4

Chickpeas don't look like they can be a satisfying snack; when you open the can or boil them, these legumes are soft and plump. Air-frying chickpeas is quick, and they turn out incredibly crispy and golden with very little oil. They are a better choice than chips or other junk food and will satisfy your craving for salt and crunch. The combination of spices in this recipe can be changed up to anything you want, or you can fry plain chickpeas accented with a little sea salt.

1 can (15 ounces, or 400 g) chickpeas, drained, rinsed, and patted dry

1 tablespoon (15 ml) olive oil, plus extra for brushing

½ teaspoon sea salt

¼ teaspoon harissa powder

¼ teaspoon garlic powder

....

1. In a medium bowl, mix together the chickpeas, oil, salt, harissa, and garlic powder.

2. Preheat the air fryer on Roast at 390°F (195°C) for 3 minutes.

3. Lightly brush the air fryer basket with oil and spread the chickpeas in a single layer. Roast for 12 minutes, tossing halfway through.

4. Cool and serve.

5. Store in an airtight container at room temperature for up to 3 days.

½ small eggplant, halved lengthwise and cut into ½-inch (1.3 cm) cubes

1 zucchini, cut into ½-inch (1.3 cm) pieces

1 red bell pepper, cut into ½-inch (1.3 cm) pieces

½ red onion, cut into ½-inch (1.3 cm) pieces

2 cloves garlic, peeled and lightly crushed

1 tablespoon (15 ml) olive oil

1 can (15 ounces, or 400 g) low-sodium chickpeas, drained and rinsed

Juice of ½ lemon

Sea salt

Freshly ground black pepper

Pita bread, cut vegetables, or tortilla chips, for serving

ROASTED VEGETABLE HUMMUS

SERVES: 4

Hummus has become a mainstream product, but if you are over a certain age, you will remember when this humble dish was only seen in specialty restaurants. What a shame it took so long for people to try this creamy, garlicky dip and even longer to start experimenting with other ingredients in their own kitchen. When you combine eggplant with the other vegetables in this recipe and air-fry them to a perfect turn, the texture is silky, and the taste is mellow and rich. Try this dip tossed with pasta if you want a simple, appetizing meal in minutes.

1. Preheat the air fryer at 375°F (190°C) for 3 minutes.

2. In a large bowl, toss the eggplant, zucchini, bell pepper, onion, garlic, and oil until the vegetables are coated.

3. Season lightly with salt and pepper and transfer them to the air fryer basket. Cook for 12 to 15 minutes, tossing once or twice, until tender and lightly caramelized.

4. Transfer the vegetables and any juices accumulated in the bottom of the air fryer into a food processor. Add the chickpeas and lemon juice and process until smooth.

5. Season with salt and pepper and serve with your preferred dippers.

6. Store the dip in a sealed container in the refrigerator for up to 4 days.

TOFU FRIES WITH CHILI LIME KETCHUP

SERVES: 2

Looking for a healthy alternative to your beloved potato fries and ketchup? Look no further than these lightly browned tofu batons for a filling snack or light meal. Air-frying the tofu ensures the finish is perfect and the amount of oil minimal. Tossing the tofu in cornstarch creates a coating that crisps up, and the added spices infuse every bite. Don't skip the homemade ketchup dipping sauce; you might want to double the recipe because it is absolutely addictive.

1. In a small bowl, whisk together the ketchup, brown sugar, balsamic vinegar, lime juice, and red pepper flakes. Transfer the ketchup to an airtight container in the refrigerator for up to 2 weeks.

2. In a small bowl, toss the cornstarch, garlic powder, oregano, basil, onion powder, paprika, and salt until well mixed.

3. In a medium bowl, gently toss the tofu fries with the olive oil. Add the seasoning mix to the tofu and toss gently until well coated.

4. Preheat the air fryer at 400°F (200°C) for 3 minutes. Lightly spray the air fryer basket with oil.

5. Working in batches, place the tofu fries in a single layer in the basket, lightly spray with oil, and cook for 10 minutes, shaking halfway through, until golden and crispy.

6. Repeat with the remaining fries and serve with the chili lime ketchup.

CHILI LIME KETCHUP

½ cup (120 g) store-bought ketchup

1 tablespoon (15 g) brown sugar

1 tablespoon (15 ml) balsamic vinegar

Juice of ½ lime

¼ teaspoon red pepper flakes

TOFU FRIES

1 tablespoon (8 g) cornstarch

1 teaspoon garlic powder

1 teaspoon dried oregano

½ teaspoon dried basil

½ teaspoon onion powder

¼ teaspoon ground paprika

¼ teaspoon sea salt

2 teaspoons olive oil

Oil spray

1 block (14 ounces, or 400 g) extra-firm tofu, pressed and cut into ½-inch (1.3 cm) batons

BUTTERMILK-HERB RANCH DRESSING

¾ cup (175 g) mayonnaise

½ cup (115 g) sour cream

¼ cup (60 ml) buttermilk

¼ cup (25 g) chopped scallions

2 tablespoons (8 g) chopped fresh dill

1 tablespoon (3 g) chopped chives

½ teaspoon garlic powder

½ teaspoon onion powder

½ teaspoon cayenne pepper

Kosher salt and pepper to taste

FRIED PICKLES

1 jar (32 ounces, or 905 g) kosher dill pickles

¾ cup (94 g) all-purpose flour

Kosher salt and pepper to taste

2½ cups (125 g) panko breadcrumbs

2 eggs beaten with 2 tablespoons (30 ml) water

Vegetable oil for spraying

FRIED PICKLES WITH BUTTERMILK-HERB RANCH DRESSING

MAKES: 32 to 36 spears or 6 to 8 servings

With a simple flour-egg-breadcrumb coating and just a spritz of oil, these fried pickles come out extra crunchy and stay that way even after they cool down. Pickle spears are easier to transfer in and out of the air fryer. Serve these fried pickles with a homemade herb-buttermilk ranch dressing and they may become one of your favorite recipes.

1. To make the dressing, in a medium bowl, whisk together the mayonnaise, sour cream, and buttermilk. Add the scallions, herbs, and seasonings and stir to combine. Cover the bowl and chill for at least 30 minutes prior to serving to allow the flavors to develop.

2. To make the fried pickles, cut each pickle into 4 spears and place the spears on paper towels to drain for at least 15 minutes. Place the flour on a plate and season with salt and pepper. Place the panko on a separate plate. Dip a pickle spear in the flour, shaking off any excess, then coat with egg mixture. Dredge the spear in the panko, pressing to make the crumbs adhere, and place the breaded spear on a lined baking sheet. Repeat with the remaining spears.

3. Spray the spears with oil and, working in batches, place them in a single layer in the air fryer basket. Cook at 400°F (200°C) for 8 to 10 minutes, flipping once halfway through. Serve with buttermilk ranch dressing.

AVOCADO CHIPOTLE DEVILED EGGS

MAKES: 12

This pale green spicy version of deviled eggs would have been shocking to a retro crowd but is very on-trend in today's culinary climate. The fact that you can make perfect hard-boiled eggs in an air fryer makes it worth buying this handy kitchen tool.

1. Place the wire rack that comes with most air fryers in the basket and place the eggs onto the rack. If you have no rack, place the eggs directly in the basket. Air Fry at 300°F (150°C) for 11 minutes.

2. Remove the eggs to a medium bowl filled with ice and water to stop the cooking process.

3. When the eggs are cool, peel them and cut them lengthwise in half.

4. Scoop out the yolks, place them in a medium bowl, and set the whites on a serving plate.

5. Add the avocado to the bowl and mash with the yolks until well blended and smooth. Stir in the mayonnaise, lemon juice, cilantro, and chili powder. Season lightly with salt and pepper.

6. Spoon the yolk mixture back into the hollows in the whites. Serve immediately or store in a sealed container in the refrigerator for up to 1 day.

6 large eggs

½ avocado

¼ cup (60 g) mayonnaise

Juice of ½ lemon

2 tablespoons (2 g) minced cilantro

¼ teaspoon chipotle chili powder

Sea salt

Freshly ground black pepper

NOTE

You can also create some interesting variations for deviled eggs, depending on the ingredients added to the yolk filling. You can keep it traditional with mayonnaise and paprika, or try chili powder, dill, curry, sun-dried tomatoes, or pesto.

1 block (8 ounces, or 225 g) cream cheese, at room temperature

½ cup (60 g) finely diced red bell pepper

¼ cup (30 g) finely diced jalapeño pepper

1 scallion, white and green parts, finely diced

1 tablespoon (1 g) finely chopped fresh cilantro

⅛ teaspoon cayenne pepper

Salt sea

Freshly ground black pepper

2 (8-inch/20 cm) flour tortillas

1 cup (120 g) shredded Cheddar cheese

Sour cream, for serving

NOTE

If you want to ensure your pinwheels do not unroll during cooking, secure them with toothpicks. Just make sure you remove them before eating!

ANTOJITOS

SERVES: 4

Antojitos means "little cravings" in Spanish. Antojitos can range from bite-size quesadillas to tamales, but these creamy, cheesy, crispy pinwheels with the slow-building heat from jalapeños and cayenne are exceptional and addictive.

1. In a medium bowl, combine the cream cheese, bell pepper, jalapeño, scallion, cilantro, and cayenne until well mixed and season with salt and pepper.

2. Place the tortillas on a clean work surface and evenly divide the filling between them. Spread the filling right to the tortilla edges and sprinkle the shredded cheese on top, dividing it between them.

3. Roll up a tortilla firmly starting at the end closest to you, placing it seam-side down as you roll the remaining tortilla. Cut a tortilla on a bias into 1½-inch (3.5 cm)-wide slices and place them in a 7-inch (18 cm) round baking pan. The end pieces will be uneven, but you can use them anyway. Cut the remaining tortilla and cover with plastic wrap so the pieces don't dry out.

4. Preheat the air fryer at 350°F (180°C) for 3 minutes.

5. Cook the tortillas for 5 to 6 minutes, or until crisp and golden. Remove and repeat with the remaining tortillas.

6. Serve with sour cream.

ROASTED GARLIC GUACAMOLE WITH HOMEMADE TORTILLA CHIPS

SERVES: 4 to 6

Roasting garlic in the air fryer is another revelation. It takes half the time of the oven. Here, roasted garlic brings a mellow sweetness to creamy guacamole with just a hint of heat from a roasted jalapeño pepper. Serve these homemade chips with soups, dips, or use them to make epic nachos. Store-bought chips pale in comparison.

....

1. To make the roasted garlic, cut off the top third of the head of garlic, exposing the tops of the cloves, and drizzle with oil. Wrap in foil and place garlic in the basket of the air fryer. Cook at 400°F (200°C) for 20 to 25 minutes until the cloves are soft. Remove the garlic from the air fryer, unwrap, and allow to cool. Squeeze the garlic cloves into a large bowl.

2. Place the jalapeño pepper in the basket of the air fryer and cook at 400°F (200°C) until the skin is blackened on all sides, turning 2 or 3 times, approximately 12 minutes. Remove the pepper and cover for 10 minutes. When the pepper is cool enough to handle, remove the charred outer skin. Remove the seeds and dice the pepper. Add to the bowl with the roasted garlic.

3. Halve the avocados and remove the pits. Scoop the avocado into the bowl with the roasted garlic and pepper. Mash together. Add the lime juice, cumin, 1 teaspoon of the salt, and cayenne pepper and stir to combine. Stir in the onion and tomatoes. Taste and adjust the seasoning. Cover the guacamole with plastic wrap and refrigerate until needed.

4. To make the tortilla chips, brush the corn tortillas with oil and sprinkle each one with ¼ teaspoon salt. Cut each tortilla into 6 wedges. Preheat the air fryer at 400°F (200°C) for 3 minutes. Working in batches, spread the tortilla chips in a single layer in the basket of the air fryer. Cook for 4 to 6 minutes, turning once halfway through, until crisp. Remove and repeat with the remaining chips. Allow the chips to cool before serving.

ROASTED GARLIC GUACAMOLE

1 head garlic

1 teaspoon vegetable oil

1 jalapeño pepper

4 ripe avocados

3 tablespoons (45 ml) freshly squeezed lime juice

1 teaspoon cumin

1 teaspoon kosher salt

Pinch cayenne pepper

½ red onion, diced

2 plum tomatoes, seeded and diced

TORTILLA CHIPS

12 corn tortillas

Vegetable oil for brushing

3 teaspoons kosher salt

CRISPY VEGETABLE SPRING ROLLS

MAKES: 14 spring rolls

These rolls are long and skinny and have a shatteringly crispy exterior. To make sure your spring rolls come out super crispy, look for 8-inch (20 cm) square frozen spring roll sheets, not the thicker, doughier egg roll wrappers, which bubble when cooked.

It is important to allow the filling to cool completely before filling the spring rolls or else they may end up soggy. You can prepare the spring rolls up to several hours in advance and keep them covered in the refrigerator until needed. But they are best enjoyed fresh out of the air fryer! Try serving them with a bottled sweet chili sauce.

2 tablespoons (30 ml) vegetable oil plus more for brushing

5 ounces (140 g) shiitake mushrooms, diced

4 cups (360 g) sliced Napa cabbage

3 carrots, cut into thin matchsticks

1 bunch scallions, white and light green parts only, sliced

1 tablespoon (10 g) minced garlic

1 tablespoon (6 g) minced fresh ginger

2 tablespoons (30 ml) soy sauce

1 package (3.75 ounces, or 106 g) bean thread noodles (also called glass or cellophane noodles)

¼ teaspoon cornstarch

1 package (12 ounces, or 340 g) frozen spring roll wrappers, defrosted according to package instructions

1. In a large skillet, heat the oil over medium-high heat until shimmering. Add the mushrooms, cabbage, and carrots and sauté until softened, about 3 minutes. Add the scallions, garlic, and ginger and sauté an additional minute or two until fragrant. Add the soy sauce and, with a wooden spoon, scrape up any browned bits on the bottom of the pan. Remove from the heat and allow to cool completely before proceeding. If any liquid has accumulated in the bottom of the pan, pour it off so the filling is not soggy.

2. Place the bean thread noodles in a bowl and pour boiling water over them. Allow to stand for 10 minutes, until softened, and then drain. Remove 1 cup (150 g) of noodles and fold them into the vegetable mixture, reserving the remainder for another use.

3. Assemble the rolls. Dissolve the cornstarch in a small dish of warm water and place it nearby. Place 1 wrapper on a clean board with a corner pointing toward you. Keep the other wrappers covered with a damp towel to prevent them from drying out while you work. Place 3 tablespoons (26 g) of filling in a line above the bottom corner, leaving space on both sides. Pick up the bottom corner and begin rolling the wrapper tightly around the filling until you reach the middle. Tightly fold in the sides and continue rolling until you reach the top corner. Dab a small bit of the water-cornstarch mixture on the top corner and seal the roll closed. Place the completed roll on a lined baking sheet and cover with a towel while you complete the remaining rolls. (Spring rolls may be frozen at this point.)

4. To cook, brush the outside of each roll lightly with oil. Working in batches of 5 at a time, place the rolls in the air fryer and cook at 400°F (200°C) for 8 to 10 minutes, flipping once halfway through. (To cook frozen rolls add 5 to 6 minutes to the cooking time.) Serve immediately with a dipping sauce.

5 ounces (140 g) lump crabmeat, drained and patted with paper towels to remove excess liquid

4 ounces (115 g) cream cheese, at room temperature

2 scallions, white and green parts only, sliced, plus more for garnish

1½ teaspoons toasted sesame oil

1 teaspoon Worcestershire sauce

Kosher salt and pepper

24 wonton wrappers (2-inch [5 cm]), thawed if frozen

3 tablespoons (45 ml) vegetable oil, for brushing

CRAB RANGOON

MAKES: 24 pieces, to serve 6 to 8

A staple of Chinese and Thai restaurant menus—although it was surely invented in America—crab rangoon is a perennial favorite. Like egg rolls and gyoza, crab rangoons come out golden and crispy in the air fryer without all the mess and oil of deep-frying. Serve these air-fried crab rangoons at your next cocktail party and watch them disappear.

Any number of dipping sauces work well with crab rangoon, from bottled sweet chili sauce to a spicy Chinese mustard. Better yet, offer all three and let your guests decide.

....

1. Combine the lump crabmeat, cream cheese, scallions, sesame oil, Worcestershire sauce, and salt and pepper to taste in a medium bowl. Stir until the mixture is completely smooth.

2. To assemble, take a wonton wrapper and place 1 scant teaspoon of filling in the center of the wrapper. (Do not overfill.) With a finger dipped in water, moisten the edges of 2 adjacent sides of the wrapper. Fold in half to form a triangle. Place the filled triangle on a plate or baking sheet lined with parchment paper. Repeat with the remaining filling until all the wonton wrappers have been filled. (Uncooked rangoons can be wrapped and kept frozen for 1 to 2 weeks. Do not thaw before cooking.)

3. Preheat the air fryer at 350°F (180°C) for 3 minutes. To cook, brush the rangoons lightly with oil on both sides and arrange in batches in the air fryer basket, 6 to 8 at a time. Cook the rangoons until crisp and golden, about 10 minutes. Garnish the cooked crab rangoons with sliced scallions and serve immediately with your favorite dipping sauce.

3

SOUPS, SANDWICHES, SALADS, AND LUNCHES

ROASTED RED PEPPER TOMATO SOUP

SERVES: 4

Red bell peppers and tomatoes become sweet and smoky when roasted, either in the oven or, in this case, an air fryer. The rich taste is deepened even further with the addition of garlic and balsamic vinegar. You can certainly substitute yellow or orange bell peppers instead, but the color will not be a luscious red. If you happen to have leftovers (unlikely!), serve them spooned over pasta with a generous sprinkle of Parmesan and fresh basil.

....

1. In a medium bowl, toss the tomatoes, bell pepper, celery, onion, garlic, oil, and vinegar until well mixed.

2. Transfer the vegetables to the air fryer basket and Air Fry at 375°F (190°C) for 15 minutes, tossing halfway through, until tender and lightly charred.

3. In a food processor or blender, purée the vegetables and any liquid in the bottom of the air fryer with the broth until smooth.

4. Transfer the soup to a large saucepan and bring to a simmer over medium heat, about 5 minutes. Whisk in the cream and basil and season with salt and pepper. Serve.

1½ pounds (680 g) tomatoes, quartered

1 red bell pepper, quartered

2 celery stalks, cut into 1-inch (2.5 cm) pieces

½ sweet onion, cut into 1-inch (2.5 cm) pieces

3 cloves garlic, smashed

2 tablespoons (30 ml) olive oil

2 tablespoons (30 ml) balsamic vinegar

2 cups (470 ml) low-sodium vegetable broth

½ cup (120 ml) coconut cream or heavy (whipping) cream

2 tablespoons (5 g) chopped fresh basil

Sea salt

Freshly ground black pepper

NOTE

Pureeing hot soup in a blender requires a few safety guidelines to avoid burning yourself. Remove the plug in the blender lid and use a thick kitchen cloth to hold the lid and cover the hole. This will let the steam escape, so the soup won't explode. Also, work in small batches so that the amount does not pulse up too high when blending.

2 parsnips, peeled and cut into 1-inch (2.5 cm) pieces

1 sweet potato, peeled and cut into 1-inch (2.5 cm) pieces

1 potato, peeled and cut into 1-inch (2.5 cm) pieces

1 carrot, peeled and cut into 1-inch (2.5 cm) pieces

½ sweet onion, chopped

1 teaspoon minced garlic

1 tablespoon (15 ml) olive oil

3 cups (705 ml) vegetable broth

1 cup (235 ml) canned coconut milk

1 teaspoon ground cumin

½ teaspoon ground coriander

Sea salt

Freshly ground black pepper

COCONUT ROASTED ROOT VEGETABLE SOUP

SERVES: 4

This is not a precise soup; inspiration can come from what you have in your refrigerator, from what you find at the store, or even from the bounty in your garden. The starchy root vegetables are sublime in the air fryer, tender and lightly browned in very little time. Try to find smaller parsnips about an inch (2.5 cm) in diameter—the large ones can be woody and slightly acrid. If you purchase the parsnips from a grocery store rather than growing them, make sure you peel or scrub them well because many growers apply a wax layer to protect the vegetables during shipping.

1. In a large bowl, toss the parsnip, sweet potato, potato, carrot, onion, garlic, and oil until well coated.

2. Place the vegetables in the air fryer basket and Air Fry at 375°F (190°C) for 20 to 25 minutes, shaking once or twice, until very tender and lightly caramelized.

3. While the vegetables are cooking, bring the broth and coconut milk to a boil in a large saucepan over medium-high heat.

4. Working in batches, if needed, transfer the vegetables to a food processor, including any liquid in the bottom of the air fryer, and add half the broth mixture. Process until the soup is very smooth, adding more broth if needed.

5. Add the puréed vegetables to the saucepan, whisking to blend with the remaining broth. Add the cumin and coriander and season to taste with salt and pepper.

6. Bring to a simmer, then serve.

RED PEPPER BLACK OLIVE QUESADILLAS

SERVES: 2

This quesadilla might seem simple, but sometimes a few distinct, strong flavors like black olives, sweet roasted peppers, and robust spinach are enough to produce something exceptional. Feel free to switch the filling up with fresh tomatoes, salsa, jalapeños, beans, or goat cheese to suit your own palate.

....

1. Preheat the air fryer at 400°F (200°C) for 3 minutes.

2. Lay 2 tortillas on a clean work surface and evenly divide the cheese between them, sprinkling it to the edges. Top them evenly with the red pepper, olives, spinach, and oregano and cover with the remaining tortillas. Press down firmly.

3. Secure the quesadillas with 2 toothpicks each and brush both sides of each quesadilla with oil. Cook one at a time for 10 minutes, flipping halfway through, until golden brown and the cheese is melted.

4. Remove the toothpicks, cut the quesadillas into quarters, and serve.

4 (6-inch/15 cm) flour tortillas

1 cup (115 g) shredded Mexican-blend cheese

½ cup (90 g) chopped jarred roasted red pepper

¼ cup (25 g) sliced black olives

1 cup (30 g) shredded baby spinach

2 tablespoons (8 g) chopped fresh oregano

Olive oil, for brushing

MANGO CHUTNEY

1 teaspoon avocado or olive oil

¼ red bell pepper, diced

¼ sweet onion, diced

1 tablespoon (10 g) minced jalapeño pepper

½ teaspoon peeled and grated fresh ginger

1 large mango, chopped

Juice and zest of ½ lime

1 teaspoon chopped fresh cilantro

Sea salt

Freshly ground black pepper

BARBECUE TOFU SANDWICHES

1 block (14 ounces, or 400 g) extra-firm tofu, pressed and cut into ¼-inch (½ cm) thick slices

1 cup (250 g) barbecue sauce, homemade or store-bought

Avocado oil, for brushing

2 crusty buns, halved lengthwise and toasted (optional)

2 cups (40 g) arugula or baby spinach

BARBECUE TOFU AND MANGO SANDWICH

SERVES: 2

If you crave the taste of barbecue, this sandwich will prove meat is not necessary to enjoy smoky, bold flavors. In the air fryer, the tofu crisps on the edges similar to grilling, and the even heat finishes the sauce to a tempting, sticky glaze. The sandwich can be served without the chutney, but the ginger and jalapeño-infused mango mixture elevates the flavor to new culinary heights. Choose ripe mangos with a perceptible fragrance through the skin; this ensures the flesh will be a vibrant yellow and the taste sweet and piney.

1. Heat the oil in a medium saucepan over medium-high heat. Sauté the bell pepper, onion, jalapeño pepper, and ginger until softened, about 3 minutes.

2. Add the mango, lime juice, and lime zest and sauté until the mixture is heated through, about 3 minutes.

3. Remove from the heat, stir in the cilantro, and season with salt and pepper. Transfer the chutney to a container, partially cover, and chill. Store in the refrigerator until you are ready to use it, up to 5 days.

4. On a large plate, coat the tofu slices with barbecue sauce on all sides.

5. Preheat the air fryer at 360°F (182°C) for 3 minutes.

6. Brush the air fryer basket with oil and arrange half the tofu slices in a single layer. Cook for 15 minutes until glazed and lightly caramelized on the edges, turning halfway through and shaking the basket several times. Repeat with the remaining tofu.

7. Pile the barbecued tofu on the buns and top with a generous scoop of the mango chutney and the arugula. Serve.

GOLDEN APPLE BRIE SANDWICH

SERVES: 2

Making sandwiches in an air fryer creates nice, crunchy bread. It's a perfect grilled cheese alternate. This sandwich is made with ripe, glossy apples, homemade jelly created from plump chile peppers, and brie. The creamy texture and rich taste of brie with tart apples makes a perfect pair. Source these sandwich ingredients from a local market for a fresh-tasting lunch.

4 thick slices bread
(sourdough or multigrain)

2 tablespoons (40 g)
hot pepper jelly

1 round brie (8 ounces,
or 225 g), cut into ¼-inch
(½ cm)-thick slices

½ tart apple, thinly sliced

2 tablespoons (28 g) butter,
at room temperature

1. Place the bread slices on a clean work surface and spread them with the hot pepper jelly. Place the brie slices on 2 pieces of bread and top with the apple slices. Evenly divide the remaining brie between the sandwiches and top with the other bread slices.

2. Preheat the air fryer at 375°F (190°C) for 3 minutes.

3. Spread the butter evenly on the top of the sandwiches and place them butter-side down in the air fryer basket. Butter the remaining side and secure the sandwiches with toothpicks.

4. Cook for 8 to 10 minutes, flipping halfway through, until golden and the cheese is melted. Remove the toothpicks and serve.

1 log (8 ounces, or 225 g) soft goat cheese, chilled

¼ cup (31 g) all-purpose flour

2 large eggs, beaten

¾ cup (90 g) breadcrumbs

Olive oil, for brushing

¼ seedless watermelon, cut into 1-inch (2.5 cm) cubes

½ cantaloupe, cut into 1-inch (2.5 cm) cubes

½ honeydew melon, cut into 1-inch (2.5 cm) cubes

¼ cup (60 ml) white balsamic vinegar

¼ cup (10 g) chiffonade fresh basil leaves

Sea salt

Freshly ground black pepper

MELON CAPRESE SALAD WITH GOLDEN GOAT CHEESE

SERVES: 4

The air-fried goat cheese is the star of this dish, but the salad also deserves a standing ovation. Although watermelon is available year-round, the best, sweetest, deepest red melons are only found in the summer.

1. Cut the goat cheese into 8 slices using fishing line or strong thread.

2. Place the flour in a small bowl, the eggs in a bowl next to the flour, and the breadcrumbs in a third bowl. Carefully dredge the goat cheese slices in the flour, then eggs, then breadcrumbs, coating the slices completely each time. Lightly brush them with oil on both sides.

3. Preheat the air fryer at 390°F (195°C) for 3 minutes.

4. Cook the cheese for 6 minutes, turning halfway through, until golden brown.

5. While the cheese is cooking, in a large bowl, toss the melon cubes, balsamic vinegar, and basil. Season lightly with salt and pepper and arrange on 4 plates. Top the salads with 2 goat cheese slices each and serve.

NOTE

You can use store-bought dressings for the salads in this book; just choose one closest to the flavors in the recipe.

ROASTED ASPARAGUS FARFALLE SALAD

SERVES: 4

Do you long for balmy evenings spent enjoying a leisurely al fresco meal on a patio or balcony? If so, this elegant salad can transport you with its earthy flavors and Mediterranean ingredients. Farfalle is used here because it's just fun; who doesn't love perky little bowties? And the scalloped edges and crevices of the shape capture all the flavors of the dressing, juices, roasted asparagus, and olives. Make sure you halve the tomatoes before air-frying them; Hot whole cherry tomatoes can burst violently when pierced by a fork.

....

1. Preheat the air fryer at 370°F (190°C) for 3 minutes.

2. In a large bowl, toss 2 tablespoons (30 ml) balsamic dressing, asparagus, and onion until well coated.

3. Transfer the vegetables to the air fryer basket and cook for 10 minutes, shaking once or twice, until tender. Add the cherry tomatoes halfway through the cooking time.

4. Transfer the vegetables to a large bowl along with any juices in the bottom of the air fryer and add the remaining dressing, farfalle, olives, Parmesan cheese, and basil and toss to combine. Serve.

½ cup (120 ml) store-bought balsamic dressing, divided

12 to 16 asparagus spears, woody ends trimmed, cut into 2-inch (5 cm) pieces

¼ red onion, cut into ½-inch (1.3 cm) chunks

20 cherry tomatoes, halved

4 cups (560 g) cooked farfalle pasta

¼ cup (40 g) sliced, pitted Kalamata olives

¼ cup (25 g) shredded Parmesan cheese

2 tablespoons (5 g) chopped fresh basil

2 (10 × 15-inch/25 × 38 cm) sheets puff pastry, thawed

6 (2 × 2 × ½-inch/5 × 5 × 1.3 cm) slices Gouda cheese

Water

2 large eggs, beaten

1 cup (115 g) breadcrumbs

Avocado oil, for brushing

DUTCH CHEESE SOUFFLÉ (KAASSOUFFLÉ)

SERVES: 6

Kaassoufflé is a Dutch snack made of melted cheese in a crispy, flaky puff pastry. It's traditionally deep-fried, but it's so easy to make in an air fryer that you'll never get splashed by hot oil again. These lovely little packets filled with melty, nutty gouda are ready in a snap. Make a few batches to serve as an appetizer at your next potluck or get-together.

....

1. Using a sharp knife or pizza roller, cut each sheet of puff pastry into 6 squares.

2. Place half of the puff pastry squares on a clean work surface and put a slice of cheese in each square's center.

3. Brush the edges of the pastry squares with water and top each with another square, pressing lightly to seal tightly.

4. Place the beaten eggs in a small bowl and the breadcrumbs in another.

5. Dredge the pastry squares in the egg and then the breadcrumbs, coating them completely.

6. Preheat the air fryer at 340°F (175°C) for 3 minutes.

7. Lightly brush the breaded squares with oil and arrange half in the air fryer basket in a single layer. Cook until puffy and golden, about 10 minutes, turning halfway through. Repeat with the remaining squares and serve.

LOADED FLATBREAD PIZZA

SERVES: 2

This flatbread crust is more flavorful than regular pizza dough, and extremely convenient. The vegetarian toppings blend into a salty, sweet, hot, nutty, and peppery symphony in the mouth, and a thin layer of pesto adds complex taste but does not overpower the rest. This dish can be made in minutes.

....

1. Preheat the air fryer at 370°F (190°C) for 3 minutes.

2. Spread the pesto on the flatbread all the way to the edges. Top the pizza with the tomato slices, artichoke hearts, and olives. Sprinkle with the red pepper flakes and the Parmesan cheese.

3. Place in the air fryer basket and cook until crispy and the cheese is melted, about 6 to 7 minutes.

4. Top with the arugula, cut into quarters, and serve.

1 (8-inch/20 cm) thin-crust flatbread

3 tablespoons (45 g) basil pesto, homemade or store-bought

1 medium tomato, thinly sliced

¼ cup (75 g) quartered marinated artichoke hearts

2 tablespoons (6 g) sliced black olives

Pinch red pepper flakes

½ cup (50 g) shaved Parmesan cheese

¼ cup (5 g) shredded arugula

4

DINNERTIME MAIN COURSES

ZUCCHINI, SPINACH, AND FETA PANCAKES WITH TZATZIKI

MAKES: 6 pancakes, to serve 3 or 4

These pancakes, with spinach, fresh herbs, and feta, are an especially satisfying and nutritious vegetarian meal. Because this dish is inspired by Greek flavors, serve it with a refreshing cucumber tzatziki as an accompaniment. Use the same herbs, or combination of herbs, in the tzatziki as in the pancakes to simplify your shopping.

Coating the zucchini with breadcrumbs helps prevent the pancakes from sticking to the air fryer as well as adds a nice crunch.

....

1. To make the tzatziki, coarsely grate the cucumber. Place the shreds in a colander and toss with 1 teaspoon of the salt. Allow to drain for at least 15 minutes. Pick up handfuls of cucumber and squeeze out the excess liquid. Place the drained shreds in a medium bowl. Add the yogurt, lemon juice, olive oil, herbs, garlic, and pepper. Stir to combine. Taste and add more salt if needed. Cover and chill for at least 1 hour to allow the flavors to develop.

2. To make the pancakes, coarsely grate the zucchini. Place the shreds in a colander and toss with the salt. Allow to drain for at least 15 minutes. Pick up handfuls of zucchini and squeeze out the excess liquid. Place the drained shreds in a medium bowl. Add the spinach, scallions, garlic, feta, herbs, flour, baking powder, and pepper and toss to combine. Pour the beaten eggs over the mixture and stir with a fork until thoroughly combined.

3. Spread the panko out on a plate. Scoop out approximately ½ cup (125 g) of the zucchini mixture and form into a 1-inch (2.5 cm)-thick oval patty with your hands. Dredge the patty in the panko. Spray both sides and the basket of the air fryer with oil. Carefully place the patty in the basket of the air fryer. Repeat twice more until you have 3 patties in the air fryer basket.

TZATZIKI

1 English or hothouse cucumber

1 teaspoon kosher salt plus more to taste

1 cup (230 g) plain Greek yogurt, preferably full-fat

2 tablespoons (30 ml) freshly squeezed lemon juice

1 tablespoon (15 ml) extra-virgin olive oil

2 teaspoons chopped fresh herbs, such as mint, dill, or oregano

2 cloves garlic, minced

½ teaspoon black pepper

ZUCCHINI PANCAKES

3 small or 2 medium zucchini

1 teaspoon kosher salt

2 cups (60 g) tightly packed baby spinach leaves, sliced

3 scallions, white and light green parts only, sliced

2 cloves garlic, minced

4 ounces (115 g) Greek feta, crumbled (about ¾ cup)

2 tablespoons (10 g) chopped fresh herbs, such as mint, dill, or oregano

⅓ cup (42 g) all-purpose flour

½ teaspoon baking powder

1 teaspoon black pepper

2 eggs, beaten

1½ cups (75 g) panko breadcrumbs

Vegetable oil for spraying

4. Cook at 375°F (190°C) until the top of the patty is browned and firm, 8 to 10 minutes. Using a silicone spatula, carefully flip the patties over and cook until the other side is well-browned, 4 to 6 minutes. Remove the cooked patties to a plate and repeat with the remaining batter, making 3 more patties.

5. Serve the zucchini pancakes hot or warm with tzatziki sauce on the side.

6 ounces (170 g) frozen chopped kale, thawed and squeezed out

¼ sweet onion, chopped

1 scallion, white and green parts, chopped

1 tablespoon (4 g) chopped fresh parsley

1 tablespoon (6 g) chopped fresh mint

1 tablespoon (15 ml) freshly squeezed lemon juice

½ teaspoon minced garlic

¾ cup (112 g) crumbled feta cheese

1 large egg, beaten

¼ teaspoon ground nutmeg

10 sheets phyllo pastry, cut in half

¼ cup (55 g) melted butter

KALE SPANAKOPITA PIE

SERVES: 4

Phyllo cooks up beautifully in the air fryer; this ingredient seems made for that cooking environment. Don't worry if the completed dish looks a little rustic with all the tucked and folded edges; it tastes delicious.

1. In a medium bowl, stir the kale, onion, scallion, parsley, mint, lemon juice, garlic, feta, egg, and nutmeg until well combined.

2. Place the phyllo sheets on a clean work surface and cover them with a clean, damp kitchen cloth.

3. Lightly grease a 7-inch (18 cm) round baking pan with butter. Place 2 sheets of phyllo in the dish, pressing them into the bottom edges. They can drape up the sides a little. Brush the top sheet with butter. Repeat until you have 10 stacked sheets.

4. Add the filling to the pan and spread it evenly over the phyllo. Layer the remaining 10 sheets, 2 at a time, brushing the top sheet with butter, until you have 10 sheets layered on the top. Trim the edges or tuck them in so there is no excess hanging over the sides. Score the top into quarters, cutting about 6 sheets into the top.

5. Preheat the air fryer at 390°F (195°C) for 3 minutes.

6. Cook for 20 to 22 minutes until crispy and golden.

7. Let cool for 10 minutes, cut the pie into quarters, and serve.

NOTE

Use any dark leafy green in place of the kale, such as spinach, the classic choice, or Swiss chard, or even a combination of greens.

EGGPLANT PAPRIKASH

SERVES: 2

As you may have guessed by the title, this recipe is a Hungarian love song dedicated to paprika, a gorgeous spice commonly used in that country's spectacular cuisine. Paprika is made from ground pods of Capsicum annuum peppers and can be found in several different types in the local grocery store. You will see plain paprika, hot, or smoked on the spice shelves; pick up whatever is recommended in your recipe (smoked in this case). The flavors of each are very different, and they are not usually interchangeable. Smoked paprika has a lush, rich flavor that is not fiery or overwhelming. It gently melds with the porous eggplant and tart sour cream in this dish, creating a sublime stew perfect for egg noodles or rice.

....

1. In a large bowl, toss the eggplant, onion, oil, and garlic, then transfer them to the air fryer basket.

2. Air Fry at 375°F (190°C) for 10 minutes, tossing once or twice, until tender.

3. Transfer the vegetables to a 7-inch (18 cm) round baking pan (3 inches/7.5 cm deep). Stir in the tomatoes and paprika and cook for 20 minutes, stirring halfway through, until the vegetables are very tender and the flavors are blended.

4. Season with salt and pepper and stir in the heavy cream and sour cream, then serve.

½ pound (227 g) eggplant, cut into 1-inch (2.5 cm) cubes

½ onion, peeled and sliced

1 tablespoon (15 ml) olive oil

1 teaspoon minced garlic

1 can (15 ounces, or 425 g) crushed tomatoes

2 tablespoons (14 g) smoked paprika

Sea salt

Freshly ground black pepper

¼ cup (60 ml) heavy (whipping) cream

2 tablespoons (30 g) sour cream

LOADED BAKED POTATOES WITH BROCCOLI AND CHEDDAR CHEESE SAUCE

SERVES: 4

Baked potatoes take over an hour to cook in the oven, and that does not even include preheating time; the air fryer can cook a baked potato to fluffy perfection in just 40 minutes.

One could simply sprinkle grated cheese over the potatoes, but it's worth a few extra minutes to make a smooth, creamy Cheddar Cheese Sauce that coats the potatoes and broccoli and makes everyone want to scrape their plate clean. This recipe makes quite a bit, so you may have cheese sauce leftover—what a shame! Reheat it and toss with cooked pasta for a quick stovetop macaroni and cheese.

4 cups (284 g) small broccoli florets (from about 2 stalks)

2 tablespoons (30 ml) vegetable oil plus more for spraying

4 russet potatoes

CHEDDAR CHEESE SAUCE

4 tablespoons (55 g) unsalted butter

¼ cup (31 g) all-purpose flour

2 cups (470 ml) milk, warmed

1 teaspoon dry mustard

Dash Worcestershire sauce

Kosher salt and pepper to taste

12 ounces (340 g) sharp Cheddar cheese, grated

4 tablespoons (55 g) unsalted butter (optional)

1. Toss the broccoli florets with 2 tablespoons (30 ml) of oil in a bowl and set aside. Rub the skins of the potatoes with a small amount of oil and prick them all over with a fork. Place the potatoes in the basket of the air fryer and cook at 400°F (200°C) until you can easily pierce the potato with a knife, 40 to 50 minutes depending on the size of the potato.

2. While the potatoes are cooking, make the cheese sauce. Melt the butter in a large, heavy saucepan. Whisk in the flour and continue to cook over low heat, whisking constantly, for 4 to 5 minutes to cook the flour. Gradually add the milk to the saucepan, whisking constantly. Raise the heat to medium and cook until the sauce begins to thicken, about 3 to 5 minutes. Remove the saucepan from the heat and add the mustard, Worcestershire sauce, salt, and pepper. Gradually add the grated Cheddar in handfuls and stir to combine. Stir until the sauce is completely smooth. Keep warm while the potatoes continue to cook.

3. When the potatoes are cooked, remove them from the basket of the air fryer. Add the broccoli florets to the basket and cook until tender and the edges begin to brown, 8 to 10 minutes.

4. To serve, split open the top of each potato and squeeze the sides to open up the inside. If desired, add a pat of butter to each potato and season with salt and pepper. Divide the broccoli florets evenly among the 4 potatoes. Spoon cheese sauce over the broccoli and potatoes and serve immediately.

2 large russet potatoes

1 teaspoon avocado oil

1 large tomato, chopped

½ cup (100 g) canned lentils, rinsed

½ cup (50 g) sliced black olives

¼ cup (30 g) pickled vegetables

¼ cup (30 g) shredded Cheddar cheese

2 tablespoons (12 g) chopped scallion, both white and green parts

2 tablespoons (30 g) sour cream

Sea salt

Freshly ground black pepper

TURKISH BAKED POTATO (KUMPIR)

SERVES: 2

Who doesn't love an easy dinner? Baked potatoes are a versatile meal option and are easy to make in an air fryer. *Kumpir* is a Turkish street food, and typical toppings include the ones in this recipe plus mushrooms, beets, tomatoes, gherkins, corn, bulgur salad, and carrot. Use this recipe as a base and add all your favorites; the potato can never be too stuffed.

1. Rub the potatoes with oil and pierce them several times with a fork. Place them in the air fryer basket and Air Fry at 400°F (200°C) until fork-tender, about 40 minutes.

2. Cut each baked potato lengthwise, creating a slit, and open it up by pressing on the ends. Use a fork to mash up the flesh in the potatoes, keeping the skin intact. Top the potatoes with the tomato, lentils, olives, pickled vegetables, cheese, scallion, and sour cream.

3. Season with salt and pepper and serve.

SWEET POTATO AND FARRO GRAIN BOWLS WITH CREAMY HERB DRESSING

MAKES: 2 grain bowls

Grain bowls are delicious and simple all-in-one meals that allow each member of the family to customize his or her own bowl. Typically composed of a grain, such as rice, farro, or barley, and topped with vegetables, protein, and dressing, grain bowls are an easy way to create a healthy meal that feels both hearty and light.

This bowl has farro, a protein- and fiber-packed ancient grain with a delicious nutty taste and slightly chewy texture. When cooked farro is toasted in the air fryer with a spritz of oil, the grains develop a crispy crust that perfectly complements their tender, nutty interior. Top the crispy farro with air-fried vegetables and your favorite vegetable protein, such as a simple fried egg, for a complete one-dish meal.

....

1. To make the Creamy Herb Dressing, combine all the dressing ingredients in a blender. Blend on medium speed until completely combined and smooth. If the dressing is too thick, add 1 to 2 tablespoons (15 to 30 ml) of water. (The dressing can be stored, covered, and refrigerated for up to 1 week.)

2. Combine the sweet potatoes, broccoli, and ½ teaspoon of the salt in a bowl with 1 teaspoon of the olive oil and toss to combine. Arrange the vegetables in a single layer in the basket of the air fryer and cook at 350°F (180°C) until the potatoes are golden brown and the broccoli is tender and starting to brown on the tops, about 8 minutes. Transfer the vegetables to a platter and keep warm.

CREAMY HERB DRESSING

½ cup (115 g) plain Greek yogurt

½ cup (8 g) fresh cilantro or (20 g) basil leaves

2 tablespoons (30 ml) extra-virgin olive oil

1 clove garlic, peeled

Juice of 1 lemon

½ teaspoon kosher salt

½ teaspoon cumin

GRAIN BOWLS

1 cup (110 g) diced sweet potatoes

2 cups (142 g) broccoli florets

1 teaspoon kosher salt, divided

2 teaspoons extra-virgin olive oil, divided

2 cups (330 g) cooked and cooled pearled farro (1 cup [195 g] of uncooked farro, prepared according to package directions)

½ small red onion, thinly sliced

1 small avocado, pitted and diced

Kosher salt and pepper to taste

3. Drizzle the cooked farro with the remaining teaspoon of olive oil and salt and toss to combine. Cut a small piece of parchment paper into a round to cover the bottom of the air fryer basket to prevent the farro grains from slipping through the basket holes. Add the farro to the basket and cook at 350°F (180°C) for 8 minutes, tossing gently halfway through to ensure that each grain is crisping, until the farro is crisp and golden.

4. Divide the farro between 2 bowls and top each with the sweet potatoes, broccoli, red onion, and avocado. Season with salt and pepper and drizzle with Creamy Herb Dressing. Serve warm or at room temperature.

2 yellow summer squash, quartered lengthwise and sliced

1 green zucchini, quartered lengthwise and sliced

½ red onion, chopped

1 tablespoon (15 ml) olive oil

1 teaspoon minced garlic

1 large tomato, chopped

½ cup (125 g) ricotta cheese

1 large egg, beaten

2 tablespoons (5 g) chopped fresh basil

Pinch red pepper flakes

3 cups (420 g) cooked rigatoni

¼ cup (20 g) shredded Parmesan cheese

SUMMER SQUASH RIGATONI BAKE

SERVES: 2

Baked pasta is a traditional comfort food, from lasagna to cannelloni to mac and cheese. This recipe features piles of summer vegetables, perfect for a leisurely meal with a fresh green salad. You might be wondering whether summer squash is the same thing as zucchini, and the short answer is that they are both summer squash, as opposed to thick-skinned golden winter squash. In this case, summer squash is the bright yellow one, usually sitting next to the green zucchini in the produce section. You can use all green if nothing else is available.

1. In a medium bowl, toss the summer squash, zucchini, onion, oil, and garlic until the vegetables are well coated. Transfer them to a 7-inch (18 cm) round baking pan (3 inches/7.5 cm deep) and Air Fry at 375°F (190°C) for 8 to 10 minutes, tossing once or twice, until tender.

2. Stir in the tomato, ricotta cheese, egg, basil, and red pepper flakes and cook 15 minutes, stirring halfway through.

3. Stir in the rigatoni and top with Parmesan cheese. Air-fry for 5 minutes until the cheese is melted and serve.

TERIYAKI SALMON AND BROCCOLI

SERVES: 2

This is the air fryer equivalent of a sheet pan dinner. Cook the salmon and broccoli together in the air fryer for a healthy, ready-all-at-once meal. Round it out with some jasmine rice if you are so inclined. If you are serving more than two, simply double the recipe and cook it in two batches. If you can find it, try this recipe with wild-caught salmon, which has a richer flavor and a deeper hue than farm-raised. Wild-caught salmon, which is in season from May through September, is leaner than farm-raised, so be sure not to overcook it. The air fryer does a better job than the oven of keeping salmon from drying out.

....

1. To make the teriyaki marinade, whisk together 2 tablespoons (30 ml) of the soy sauce, the rice vinegar, brown sugar, and ginger in a small bowl until the sugar is dissolved. Slowly pour in ¼ cup (60 ml) of oil in a steady stream while whisking. Place the salmon fillets in a small glass baking dish and cover with the marinade. Cover and refrigerate for at least 15 minutes but no more than a half hour.

2. Meanwhile, toss the broccoli florets with the remaining soy sauce and oil and the red pepper flakes. Season with salt and pepper. Place the broccoli florets in a single layer in the basket of the air fryer. Place the salmon fillets on top of or nestled alongside the broccoli, skin-side down. Cook at 375°F (190°C) for 8 to 10 minutes until the broccoli is tender and charred and the salmon flakes easily with a fork. (Wild-caught salmon should be cooked to an internal temperature of 120°F [49°C].) Serve immediately.

¼ cup (60 ml)
soy sauce, divided

2 tablespoons (30 ml)
rice vinegar

1 tablespoon (15 g)
brown sugar

¼ teaspoon grated
fresh ginger

¼ cup (60 ml) plus
1 tablespoon (15 ml)
vegetable oil, divided

2 skin-on salmon fillets
(6 ounces or 170 g each),
at least 1 inch (2.5 cm) thick

6 cups (approximately 1 pound
[455 g]) broccoli florets

Pinch red pepper flakes

Kosher salt and pepper
to taste

FRIED FISH

1 pound (455 g) tilapia fillets (or other mild white fish)

½ cup (63 g) all-purpose flour

1 teaspoon garlic powder

1 teaspoon kosher salt

¼ teaspoon cayenne pepper

½ cup (115 g) mayonnaise

3 tablespoons (45 ml) milk

1¾ cups (89 g) panko breadcrumbs

Vegetable oil for spraying

TACOS

8 corn tortillas

¼ head red or green cabbage, shredded

1 ripe avocado, halved and each half cut into 4 slices

12 ounces (340 g) pico de gallo or other fresh salsa

Mexican crema

1 lime, cut into wedges

BAJA FISH TACOS

MAKES: 8 tacos, to serve 4

Fish tacos originated on the Baja Peninsula of Mexico sometime in the last century but have since spread all over North America. The basic version—and arguably the best—consists of nothing more than battered and fried white fish wrapped in a corn tortilla—or two for more stability—topped with a few shreds of cabbage, some pico de gallo, a dollop of creamy sauce, and an essential spritz of lime. This version hews pretty close to the classic recipe with the primary difference being that these fillets are air-fried, not deep-fried, but they are no less delectably crispy. The secret is the mayonnaise-based batter, which keeps the fish tender and moist. Use freshly made pico de gallo or a tropical fruit–based salsa to top your tacos. Elotes (page 98) would make an excellent accompaniment.

1. To make the fish, cut the fish fillets into strips 3 to 4 inches (7.5 to 10 cm) long and 1 inch (2.5 cm) wide. Combine the flour, garlic powder, salt, and cayenne pepper on a plate and whisk to combine. In a shallow bowl, whisk the mayonnaise and milk together. Place the panko on a separate plate. Dredge the fish strips in the seasoned flour, shaking off any excess. Dip the strips in the mayonnaise mixture, coating them completely, then dredge in the panko, shaking off any excess. Place the fish strips on a plate or rack.

2. Working in batches, spray half the fish strips with oil and arrange them in the basket of the air fryer, taking care not to crowd them. Cook at 400°F (200°C) for 4 minutes, then flip and cook for another 3 to 4 minutes until the outside is brown and crisp and the inside is opaque and flakes easily with a fork. Repeat with the remaining strips.

3. Heat the tortillas in the microwave or on the stovetop. To assemble the tacos, place 2 fish strips inside each tortilla. Top with shredded cabbage, a slice of avocado, pico de gallo, and a dollop of crema. Serve with a lime wedge on the side.

BUTTERMILK FRIED CHICKEN AND WAFFLES

SERVES: 4

This meal is all about having fun with your countertop appliances. Make fried chicken tenders in the air fryer and tasty buttermilk waffles in the waffle iron. Serve the chicken atop the waffles and pass the maple syrup and hot sauce!

The hardest thing about this recipe is timing the two elements. The chicken takes 15 to 20 minutes in the air fryer and needs only to be flipped once. Making waffles in a waffle iron, on the other hand, requires your constant attention. If you are good at multitasking, make the waffles while the chicken cooks. If not, make the chicken first and keep it warm in the air fryer at a low temperature while you make the waffles.

....

1. To make the chicken, cut each chicken breast in half lengthwise to make 2 long chicken tenders. Whisk together the flour, salt, and cayenne pepper on a large plate. Beat the egg with the buttermilk and hot sauce in a large, shallow bowl. Place the panko in a separate shallow bowl or pie plate.

2. Dredge the chicken tenders in the flour, shaking off any excess, then dip them in the egg mixture. Dredge the chicken tenders in the panko, making sure to coat them completely. Shake off any excess panko. Place the battered chicken tenders on a plate.

3. Preheat the air fryer at 375°F (190°C) for 3 minutes. Spray the basket lightly with oil. Arrange half the chicken tenders in the basket of the air fryer and spray the tops with oil. Cook until the top side of the tenders is browned and crispy, 8 to 10 minutes. Flip the tenders and spray the second side with oil. Cook until the second side is browned and crispy and the internal temperature reaches 165°F (71°C), another 8 to 10 minutes. Remove the first batch of tenders and keep it warm. Cook the second batch in the same manner.

FRIED CHICKEN

4 small boneless, skinless chicken breasts totaling approximately 2 pounds (910 g)

½ cup (63 g) all-purpose flour

1 teaspoon kosher salt

½ teaspoon cayenne pepper

1 egg

2 tablespoons (30 ml) buttermilk

Dash hot sauce

1½ cups (75 g) panko breadcrumbs

Vegetable oil for spraying

BUTTERMILK WAFFLES

1¾ cups (219 g) all-purpose flour

2 teaspoons baking powder

1 teaspoon granulated sugar

1 teaspoon baking soda

1 teaspoon kosher salt

1¾ cups (420 ml) buttermilk

2 eggs

½ cup (112 g, or 1 stick) unsalted butter, melted and cooled

Maple syrup or honey to serve

4. While the tenders are cooking, make the waffles. In a large bowl, whisk together the flour, baking powder, sugar, baking soda, and salt. In a separate bowl, whisk together the buttermilk, eggs, and melted butter, reserving a small amount of butter to brush on the waffle iron. Add the wet ingredients to the dry ingredients and stir with a fork until just combined. Allow the batter to rest for at least 5 minutes. Brush the waffle iron with reserved melted butter and preheat according to the manufacturer's instructions. Scoop ⅓ to ½ cup (85 to 125 g) of batter into each grid of the waffle iron and cook according to your waffle iron's instructions. (You should be able to make 8 waffles.)

5. To serve, place 2 chicken tenders on top of 1 or 2 waffles, depending on the person's appetite. Serve with maple syrup or honey and additional hot sauce.

1½ pounds (680 g) hand-filleted boneless, skinless chicken breast or regular boneless, skinless chicken breast pounded to ¼-inch (6 mm) thickness

4 cloves garlic, peeled

1 piece (1 inch [2.5 cm]) fresh ginger, peeled

1 cup (230 g) plain yogurt, preferably full fat

½ teaspoon cumin

½ teaspoon coriander

½ teaspoon ginger

¼ teaspoon paprika

¼ teaspoon cayenne pepper

¼ teaspoon turmeric

1 teaspoon kosher salt

Juice and zest of 1 lime plus more for serving

Vegetable oil for spraying

TANDOORI-STYLE CHICKEN SKEWERS

SERVES: 4

Technically speaking, tandoori chicken is chicken that has been marinated in a mixture of yogurt and spices and cooked in a super-hot clay tandoor oven. That is why this dish of chicken marinated in a mixture of yogurt and spices and cooked in the air fryer is called tandoori-style chicken. But no matter what you call it, everyone will enjoy these flavorful, juicy chicken skewers, which cook in just 10 minutes.

In earlier times, the yogurt in the tandoori marinade not only flavored the chicken but also tenderized it. The chicken we buy today is already plenty tender, which means the marinating time can be as short as 20 minutes—just long enough to flavor the chicken. Whip up a quick-cooking vegetable side dish, such Roasted Cherry Tomatoes with Basil (page 102), and dinner is on the table in a flash. Some coconut rice or warm naan would round out the meal perfectly.

1. Cut the chicken breast into strips approximately 1 inch (2.5 cm) wide and place in a glass baking dish. Mince the garlic and ginger together very finely to form a chunky paste. Whisk the garlic-ginger paste with the yogurt, spices, salt, and lime zest and juice in a medium bowl until combined. Pour the yogurt mixture into the baking dish with the chicken and turn the chicken pieces until they are coated. Cover the dish and refrigerate at least 20 minutes and up to 6 hours.

2. Preheat the air fryer at 400°F (200°C) for 3 minutes. If desired, thread half the chicken pieces onto metal skewers designed for the air fryer and place them on a rack. Alternatively, you can simply spray the air fryer basket with oil to prevent sticking and lay half the chicken pieces in the basket. Cook for 10 minutes, turning once halfway through. Repeat with the remaining chicken pieces.

3. Serve immediately with additional lime wedges for spritzing.

MUSHROOM TURKEY BURGERS

SERVES: 4

Too often, turkey burgers are dry and tasteless, making you wish you had just made regular hamburgers. To combat that, blend dark-meat ground turkey—much more flavorful than ground turkey breast—with chopped sautéed mushrooms, which add both moisture and flavor to the meat. Sautéing the mushrooms adds an extra step, but the results are worth it. Fortunately, the burgers themselves cook up quickly in the air fryer.

If your family likes cheeseburgers, after the burgers are cooked, add a slice of cheese to each burger, pressing down to ensure that it doesn't blow off in the air fryer, and cook for an additional minute.

....

1 tablespoon (14 g) unsalted butter or (15 ml) extra-virgin olive oil

8 ounces (225 g) sliced mushrooms

1½ teaspoons kosher salt, divided

1 pound (455 g) ground dark-meat turkey

½ onion, grated

1 tablespoon (15 ml) Worcestershire sauce

1 teaspoon garlic powder

1 teaspoon black pepper

Vegetable oil for spraying

4 hamburger buns

1. Heat the butter in a large, heavy skillet over medium-high heat. Add the mushrooms and arrange in a single layer. Cook the mushrooms without stirring for 2 minutes. Stir and cook for 1 to 2 minutes more. Reduce the heat and continue to sauté until the mushrooms are no longer giving off liquid, about 5 minutes. Season with ½ teaspoon salt and remove from the heat. Finely mince the mushrooms or chop them in a food processor.

2. In a large bowl, combine the minced mushrooms, turkey, onion, Worcestershire, garlic powder, the remaining salt, and pepper. Divide the mixture into 4 equal patties and using your finger, create a small depression in the middle of each patty.

3. Spray the patties and the basket of the air fryer with oil to prevent sticking. Cook the patties at 375°F (190°C) until browned and the internal temperature registers 165°F (71°C), about 15 minutes. Remove the burgers from the air fryer. Serve on buns garnished with your favorite burger toppings.

3 tablespoons (21 g) ground cumin

1 teaspoon chili powder

1 teaspoon kosher salt

¼ teaspoon black pepper

2 cloves garlic, minced

1 pound (455 g) pork tenderloin, cut into 2 pieces

Vegetable oil for spraying

1 pound (455 g) Yukon gold potatoes, quartered

1 tablespoon (15 ml) extra-virgin olive oil

CUMIN-CRUSTED PORK TENDERLOIN AND POTATOES

SERVES: 4 to 6

This easy, spice-crusted pork tenderloin with potatoes is an all-in-one dinner that is ideal for busy weekday evenings. The tenderloin cooks in just 20 minutes in the air fryer and the potatoes cook while the pork rests. Whip up a green salad and you have a complete meal that is ready in less than 30 minutes.

1. Combine the spices and garlic in a small bowl. Transfer 1 tablespoon (8 g) of the spice mixture to another bowl and set it aside to season the potatoes. Rub both pieces of the tenderloin with the remaining seasoning mixture. Set aside.

2. Preheat the air fryer at 350°F (180°C) for 3 minutes. Spray the air fryer basket with oil. Place both pieces of tenderloin in the air fryer basket and spray lightly with oil. Cook the tenderloin for approximately 20 minutes, turning halfway through, until a thermometer inserted in the center of the tenderloin reads 145°F (63°C). While the tenderloin cooks, place the potatoes in a medium bowl. Add the reserved tablespoon (8 g) of seasoning mixture and the olive oil. Toss gently to coat the potatoes.

3. Transfer the tenderloin pieces to a platter and tent with foil to rest for 10 minutes. While the tenderloin rests, place the potatoes in the air fryer. Increase the air fryer temperature to 400°F (200°C) and cook the potatoes for 8 to 10 minutes, tossing once halfway through cooking, until golden brown. Serve immediately alongside the pork tenderloin.

COUNTRY-FRIED STEAK WITH ONION GRAVY

SERVES: 4

Country-fried steak, also known as chicken-fried steak, is the very definition of a guilty pleasure. Unless, of course, you make it in the air fryer, in which case it is nearly guilt-free. Start with tenderized cube steaks for best results. The only thing better than country-fried steak is country-fried steak smothered in gravy. If you have ever been intimidated by making gravy, this no-fail method, made with basic pantry ingredients, will turn you into a gravy expert.

....

1. To make the onion gravy, melt the butter and oil in a large skillet over medium heat. Add the onion and season with salt and pepper. Sauté the onion over medium to medium-low heat, stirring occasionally, until softened and browned, approximately 15 minutes. Sprinkle the flour over the onion and stir to combine. Sauté for an additional 2 minutes until the flour smells toasty. While stirring, slowly pour in the warm chicken broth and Worcestershire sauce. Use your spoon to scrape up any brown bits that have accumulated on the bottom. Simmer the gravy until thickened, stirring frequently, 8 to 10 minutes. Taste and adjust the seasoning. Keep warm over a very low flame while you make the steaks.

2. To make the steaks, whisk together the flour, salt, pepper, and onion and garlic powders in a shallow pie plate or dish. In a second shallow dish, beat together the egg and milk. Spread the panko on a third plate or dish. Dredge a cube steak in the flour, shaking off any excess. Next, coat the steak with the egg-milk mixture. Finally, dredge the steak in the panko, shaking off any excess. Place the coated steak on a rack or plate. Repeat with the remaining steaks.

3. Preheat the air fryer at 375°F (190°C) for 3 minutes. Place 2 of the steaks in the air fryer and cook for 12 to 14 minutes, flipping once halfway through, until browned and crispy. Remove the steaks and keep warm while you cook the remaining 2 steaks in the same manner. Serve the steaks topped with onion gravy.

ONION GRAVY

1 tablespoon (14 g) unsalted butter

1 tablespoon (15 ml) vegetable oil

1 yellow onion, thinly sliced

Kosher salt and pepper to taste

2 tablespoons (16 g) all-purpose flour

2 cups (470 ml) chicken broth, warmed

½ teaspoon Worcestershire sauce

COUNTRY-FRIED STEAK

½ cup (63 g) all-purpose flour

1 teaspoon kosher salt

½ teaspoon black pepper

½ teaspoon onion powder

½ teaspoon garlic powder

1 egg

¼ cup (60 ml) milk

1½ cups (75 g) panko breadcrumbs

4 cube steaks (4 ounces, or 115 g each)

5

SIDES AND VEGETABLE DISHES

ELOTES (MEXICAN STREET CORN)

SERVES: 4 as a side dish

Does your local taqueria serve *elotes*, or have you ever been at a street festival and spied this grilled Mexican corn slathered with a creamy sauce and topped with crumbled cheese? Serve these air fryer elotes alongside your favorite Mexican-inspired meals and Taco Tuesday will never be the same!

Crema is a smooth, velvety Mexican condiment that is made by culturing heavy cream with buttermilk and seasoning it with lime and salt. It is similar to sour cream in tanginess but thinner in consistency. It is readily available in the dairy section of most stores, but, in a pinch, you can use sour cream that you have thinned with a little cream or buttermilk. You can also make crema at home, but it will take several hours to set up at room temperature.

¼ cup (60 ml) Mexican crema

¼ cup (60 g) mayonnaise

Juice and zest of 1 lime

½ teaspoon garlic powder

Pinch cayenne pepper plus more for garnish

4 shucked ears corn

2 tablespoons (28 g) unsalted butter, melted

¼ cup (38 g) crumbled queso fresco (Mexican fresh cheese)

¼ cup (4 g) chopped cilantro

....

1. Whisk together the crema, mayonnaise, lime zest, garlic powder, and a pinch of the cayenne pepper in a small bowl. Set aside.

2. Preheat the air fryer at 400°F (200°C) for 3 minutes. Brush the ears of corn with the melted butter. Place the corn in the air fryer and cook, rotating 2 or 3 times, until browned on all sides, 10 to 12 minutes. Remove the ears of corn to a serving platter.

3. Brush the ears with the crema and mayonnaise mixture. Sprinkle the crumbled queso fresco and chopped cilantro on top of the corn. Spritz the corn with the juice from the lime and sprinkle with additional cayenne pepper, if desired. Serve immediately.

1 cup (50 g) panko
breadcrumbs

1 teaspoon kosher salt
plus more for sprinkling

1 teaspoon garlic powder

1/2 teaspoon cayenne pepper

2 ripe but firm avocados

1 egg beaten with 1 tablespoon
(15 ml) water

Vegetable oil for spraying

Pomegranate molasses for
serving (optional)

AVOCADO FRIES WITH POMEGRANATE MOLASSES

MAKES: 16 fries, to serve 4

For best results, look for ripe but still firm avocados that won't fall apart when sliced. Even firm avocados can break if you try to dip them like a french fry, so drizzle these avocado fries with a thin sauce. Try pomegranate molasses, which is nothing more than pomegranate juice that has been reduced and thickened to a syrup. Look for it with other Middle Eastern ingredients at your grocery store. If you don't have pomegranate molasses, a good balsamic vinegar works as well.

1. Whisk together the panko, salt, and spices on a plate. Cut each avocado in half and remove the pit. Cut each avocado half into 4 slices and scoop the slices out with a large spoon, taking care to keep the slices intact.

2. Dip each avocado slice in the egg wash and then dredge it in the panko. Place the breaded avocado slices on a plate. Working in 2 batches, arrange half of the avocado slices in a single layer in the basket of the air fryer. Spray lightly with oil. Cook the slices for 7 to 8 minutes at 375°F (190°C), turning once halfway through. Remove the cooked slices to a platter and repeat with the remaining avocado slices.

3. Sprinkle the warm avocado slices with salt and drizzle with pomegranate molasses, if using.

ROASTED CHERRY TOMATOES WITH BASIL

SERVES: 4 as a side dish

This is one of the easiest side dishes you can make in the air fryer, and the results are spectacular. Small cherry or grape tomatoes—which are readily available year-round—become sweet, caramelized, and jammy after only 30 minutes in the air fryer. Have a picky eater who doesn't like vegetables? These may just convert them.

You will find no end of uses for these roasted tomatoes. On their own, they work as a vegetable side dish alongside grilled chicken or steak. But you can also toss them with warm pasta as a sort of chunky sauce or spoon them over crusty bread to make crostini. They are absolute heaven on scrambled eggs. Add some fresh mozzarella and you have a year-round version of a caprese salad.

....

1. Toss the tomatoes with the olive oil and salt in a medium bowl. Place as many tomatoes as will fit in the air fryer basket without crowding. For larger air fryers, this will be both pints, but smaller appliances may only fit 1 or 1½ pints. If you are not able to fit both pints in the air fryer at the beginning of cooking, add any remaining tomatoes to the basket after the first 10 minutes.

2. Cook the tomatoes at 250°F (120°C) for 30 minutes, shaking once or twice, until the tomatoes are softened and browned in places. Some tomatoes may have split or burst. Remove the tomatoes and place in a serving dish.

3. Remove the leaves from the sprig of basil and cut them into ribbons. Add the basil to the tomatoes. Serve warm or at room temperature.

2 pints (600 g) cherry or grape tomatoes

2 teaspoons extra-virgin olive oil

¼ teaspoon kosher salt

1 sprig basil

NOTE
....

In general, it is not recommended to use extra-virgin olive oil in your air fryer because EVOO has a low smoke point and typically we cook food at high temperatures in the air fryer. In this recipe, however, the temperature of the air fryer stays at a low 250°F (120°C), which is well below the smoke point for extra-virgin olive oil.

1 small head cauliflower, cut into small florets

2 teaspoons olive oil

¼ teaspoon onion powder

¼ teaspoon garlic powder

½ cup (60 g) shredded Cheddar cheese

Freshly ground black pepper

1 tablespoon (4 g) chopped fresh parsley

CHEESY CAULIFLOWER BAKE

SERVES: 4

Typically, cauliflower needs to be tender but not mushy, and the sauce requires supervision and another pot, so more dishes. So inconvenient! But you can make a very similar cheesy recipe in less than 30 minutes in the air fryer with no supervision or pile of dishes. Try your favorite nondairy cheese for a tasty vegan option.

1. Preheat the air fryer at 375°F (190°C) for 3 minutes.

2. In a medium bowl, toss the cauliflower, oil, onion powder, and garlic powder until well coated.

3. Transfer the cauliflower to the air fryer basket and cook for 12 minutes until lightly caramelized and tender, tossing halfway through.

4. Transfer the cauliflower to a 7-inch (18 cm) round baking pan and top with the cheese. Cook for 5 minutes until the cheese is melted.

5. Season with pepper and serve topped with parsley.

ASIAN VEGETABLE PACKET

SERVES: 2

Cooking different ingredients in packets, with either foil or the traditional parchment paper, is a French method called en papillote. The benefit of this preparation is all the flavors and juices stay in the packet, so the finished dish is packed with delightful taste and moistness. Air-frying ensures even heat and quick cooking time, so these soy, ginger, and honey–accented veggies turn out perfect every time. Just take care when opening the packet because the escaping steam can burn.

....

1. Drape 2 pieces of aluminum foil in a 7-inch (18 cm) round baking pan, one on top of each other in a cross. The entire pan should be covered.

2. Place the bok choy, bell pepper, scallion, broccoli, corn, and snow peas in the baking pan, tossing to combine.

3. In a small bowl, stir together the soy sauce, honey, ginger, garlic, and red pepper flakes. Drizzle it evenly over the vegetables. Fold the foil up around the vegetables to form a tightly sealed packet.

4. Preheat the air fryer on Roast at 350°F (180°C) for 3 minutes.

5. Cook for 15 minutes until the vegetables are tender.

6. Open the packet carefully to avoid the escaping steam, garnish with sesame seeds, and serve.

4 small bok choy heads, quartered

1 red bell pepper, cut into 1-inch (2.5 cm) pieces

1 scallion, white and green parts, sliced

1 cup (70 g) broccoli florets

1 cup (200 g) canned baby corn, cut into 2-inch (5 cm) pieces

1 cup (100 g) snow peas, stringed and halved

2 tablespoons (30 ml) low-sodium soy sauce

2 tablespoons (40 g) honey

1 teaspoon peeled and grated fresh ginger

½ teaspoon minced garlic

Pinch of red pepper flakes

1 teaspoon sesame seeds, for garnish

6

SWEETS AND DESSERTS

PROFITEROLES

MAKES: 8 to 10 profiteroles, to serve 4 or 5

A staple of French bistro dessert menus, profiteroles are composed of choux buns—the same kind used for cream puffs—filled with ice cream and topped with a rich chocolate sauce.

These easy air fryer profiteroles are such a fun way to end a dinner party. They look elegant but are nothing more than a dressed-up ice cream sundae.

....

1. Combine the butter, sugar, and water in a medium saucepan and melt the butter over low heat. Add the flour and stir to form a cohesive dough. Cook over medium-low heat for 2 minutes to get rid of the raw flour taste. Remove from the heat and allow to cool to room temperature. Beat the eggs in one at a time, making sure the first egg is fully incorporated before adding the second. The dough will look curdled at first, but keep beating vigorously until the dough becomes smooth. Once the eggs are fully incorporated, let the dough rest for 30 minutes.

2. While the dough is resting, make the chocolate sauce. Place the chopped chocolate and butter in a heat-proof bowl. Heat the cream and corn syrup in a small saucepan over medium heat until the cream is simmering. Remove from the heat and pour the cream mixture over the chocolate in the bowl. Stir until the chocolate and butter have melted and the sauce is smooth. Set aside.

3. Once the dough has rested, place it in a piping bag outfitted with a large, round tip. Lightly oil the basket of the air fryer. Working in 2 batches, pipe round puffs of dough approximately 2 inches (5 cm) wide and 1 inch (2.5 cm) tall directly onto the basket of the air fryer. Use a knife or scissors to cut the dough when you have achieved the desired size. With a damp finger, press down on the swirl at the top of each puff to round it. Cook at 360°F (182°C) for 18 to 20 minutes until the outside of the puffs is golden brown and crisp and the inside is fully cooked and airy.

4. To serve, halve the choux puffs crosswise and place a scoop of ice cream inside. Replace the top of the puff and spoon chocolate sauce over the top.

CHOUX PUFFS

3 tablespoons (45 g) unsalted butter

1 tablespoon (13 g) granulated sugar

1 cup (235 ml) water

1 cup (125 g) all-purpose flour

2 eggs

Vegetable oil for brushing

CHOCOLATE SAUCE

4 ounces (115 g) semisweet chocolate, finely chopped

2 tablespoons (28 g) unsalted butter, at room temperature

1 cup (235 ml) heavy cream

¼ cup (85 g) corn syrup

1 pint (285 g) vanilla ice cream for serving

CHURROS WITH CHOCOLATE DIPPING SAUCE

MAKES: 12 to 14 churros, to serve 4

Churros are another deep-fried treat that few people attempt to make at home—for all the usual reasons. But with the air fryer, it is easy to make homemade churros with only a few modifications to the traditional recipe and a fraction of the fat.

When you buy churros on the street in Spain or Latin America, they are often long and sometimes even curved into a large teardrop. To fit the air fryer, these churros are shorter—more like churro bites. But don't change one important tradition: Serve these cinnamon-dusted churros with a chocolate dipping sauce for a very special dessert.

....

1. To make the chocolate sauce, place the chopped chocolate in a heat-proof bowl. Combine the cream and corn syrup in a small saucepan and bring to a simmer. Pour the warm cream mixture over the chocolate and stir until the chocolate is melted. Add the cinnamon and cayenne pepper. Set aside.

2. To make the churros, combine 1 tablespoon (14 g) of the butter, the water, 1 tablespoon (13 g) of the sugar, and the salt in a medium saucepan. Melt the butter over low heat. Add the flour and stir vigorously to form a dough ball. Continue to cook, stirring until the mixture looks dry and thick, 2 minutes. Remove from the heat and allow to cool to room temperature. Once cool, beat in the eggs one at a time, making sure the first egg is fully incorporated before adding the second. Continue beating until the mixture is smooth. Let the dough rest for 30 minutes.

3. Place the churro batter into a piping bag outfitted with an extra-large tip, round or star-shaped. Spray the basket of the air fryer with oil. Working in batches, pipe churros that are 5 to 6 inches (13 to 15 cm) long and ¾ to 1 inch (2 to 2.5 cm) in diameter directly onto the air fryer basket. Do not crowd the basket. Use a knife or scissors to cut the dough when you've reached the desired length. Spray the churros with oil.

CHOCOLATE SAUCE

4 ounces (115 g) semisweet chocolate, finely chopped

½ cup (120 ml) heavy cream

¼ cup (85 g) light corn syrup

½ teaspoon cinnamon

¼ teaspoon cayenne pepper

CHURROS

3 tablespoons (45 g) unsalted butter, divided

1 cup (235 ml) water

½ cup (100 g) granulated sugar plus 1 tablespoon (13 g), divided

Pinch kosher salt

1 cup (125 g) all-purpose flour

2 eggs

Vegetable oil for spraying

2 teaspoons cinnamon

4. Cook at 360°F (182°C) for 12 to 14 minutes until the outside is firm and brown and the inside is soft. While the churros are cooking, combine the remaining ½ cup (100 g) sugar with the cinnamon on a plate and whisk to combine. Melt the remaining 2 tablespoons (30 g) of butter and place in a small dish.

5. Remove the cooked churros from the air fryer and immediately brush with melted butter and dredge in the cinnamon sugar. Repeat the process with the remaining churros. Serve hot with the chocolate sauce.

1 stick (4 ounces, or 112 g) unsalted butter, softened

3 tablespoons (39 g) granulated sugar

3 tablespoons (28.5 g) brown sugar

1 egg

1 teaspoon vanilla extract

½ cup (63 g) all-purpose flour

¼ teaspoon baking soda

¼ teaspoon kosher salt

½ cup (88 g) semisweet chocolate chips

Vegetable oil for spraying

Vanilla ice cream for serving

Hot fudge or caramel sauce for serving

CHOCOLATE CHIP PAN COOKIE SUNDAE

SERVES: 4

This chocolate chip pan cookie comes together quickly and with just one bowl! You can decide to make it on the spur of the moment—right before sitting down to dinner, for example—and 25 minutes later, your family will be digging into a warm, gooey pan cookie topped with vanilla ice cream and hot fudge. What a special way to keep everyone at the table a little longer. This is an easy, forgiving recipe that kids and teens can make by themselves when they have friends over.

1. In a medium bowl, cream the butter and sugars together using a handheld mixer until light and fluffy. Add the egg and vanilla and mix until combined. In a small bowl, whisk together the flour, baking soda, and salt. Add the dry ingredients to the batter and mix until combined. Add the chocolate chips and mix a final time.

2. Preheat the air fryer at 325°F (170°C) for 3 minutes. Lightly grease a 7-inch (18 cm) pizza pan insert for the air fryer. Spread the batter evenly in the pan. Place the pan in the air fryer and cook for 12 to 15 minutes, until the top of the cookie is browned and the middle is gooey but cooked. Remove the pan from the air fryer.

3. Place 1 to 2 scoops of vanilla ice cream in the center of the cookie and top with hot fudge or caramel sauce, as you prefer. Pass around spoons and eat the cookie sundae right out of the pan.

FRIED SESAME BANANAS

SERVES: 4

These are not quite fritters, more like bananas wrapped in crunchy sesame honey cookies. The sweetness of the banana is balanced by the nutty, toasty flavor of the seeds. Air-frying these exotic nuggets creates a lovely breading and pleasing soft texture in the fruit. It is best to wait before eating them because the sweet banana filling can be scalding!

....

1. In a medium bowl, stir together the flour, sesame seeds, confectioners' sugar, and salt.

2. In a small bowl, stir together the egg and water until well blended.

3. Dredge the banana chunks in the sesame mixture, then the egg, and then the sesame mixture again, using your fingers to press the breading onto the fruit. Place the breaded chunks on a plate until all the banana is coated.

4. Preheat the air fryer at 370°F (190°C) for 3 minutes.

5. Working in batches, place the banana chunks in a single layer in the air fryer basket and spray each piece with oil or melted butter.

6. Cook for 8 to 10 minutes, turning halfway through, until golden brown. Repeat with the remaining banana.

7. Let stand for at least 10 minutes and serve drizzled generously with honey.

½ cup (80 g) rice flour

½ cup (72 g) sesame seeds

1 tablespoon (7 g) confectioners' sugar

Pinch sea salt

1 large egg

2 tablespoons (30 ml) water

3 bananas, cut into 1-inch (2.5 cm) slices

Oil spray

Honey, for serving

1 pineapple

4 tablespoons (55 g) unsalted butter, melted

2 tablespoons (30 g) plus 2 teaspoons brown sugar

2 tablespoons (12 g) fresh mint, cut into ribbons

1 lime

CARAMELIZED PINEAPPLE WITH MINT AND LIME

SERVES: 4

Raw pineapple is fine, especially if you happen to be enjoying some on a Hawaiian beach. But for me, pineapple realizes its full potential when it is grilled or roasted so that it softens and the fruit's natural sugars are concentrated. The air fryer makes it simple to caramelize pineapple with just a light kiss of butter and a sprinkle of brown sugar.

Cutting the pineapple into rings before caramelizing it makes this extremely simple, tropical-inspired dish pretty enough for a party. Enjoy air-fried pineapple on its own as a light summer dessert or, if you are feeling more indulgent, add a scoop of vanilla ice cream or coconut whipped cream.

1. Cut off the top and bottom of the pineapple and stand it on a cut end. Slice off the outer skin, cutting deeply enough to remove the eyes of the pineapple. Cut off any pointy edges to make the pineapple nice and round. Cut the peeled pineapple into 8 circles, approximately ½ to ¾ inch (1.3 to 2 cm) thick. Remove the core of each slice using a small, circular cookie or biscuit cutter, or simply cut out the core using a paring knife. Place the pineapple rings on a plate.

2. Brush both sides of the pineapple rings with the melted butter. Working in 2 batches, arrange 4 slices in a single layer in the basket of the air fryer. Sprinkle ½ teaspoon brown sugar on the top of each ring. Cook at 400°F (200°C) until the top side is browned and caramelized, about 10 minutes. With tongs, carefully flip each ring and sprinkle brown sugar on the second side. Cook for an additional 5 minutes until the second side is browned and caramelized. Remove the cooked pineapple and repeat with the remaining pineapple rings.

3. Arrange all the cooked pineapple rings on a serving plate or platter. Sprinkle with mint and spritz with the juice of the lime. Serve warm.

CARAMELIZED PEACH SHORTCAKES

SERVES: 4

If strawberry shortcake knew about caramelized peach shortcake, it would retire. Luscious summer peaches with just a hint of caramelization are the perfect foil for a not-too-sweet biscuit and some whipped cream. You can also try this same method of caramelizing fruit in the air fryer with other stone fruits, such as nectarines and apricots—whatever looks good at the farmers market!

For convenience, you can make the biscuits and the whipped cream in advance. The peaches are best served warm.

1. To make the shortcakes, place the flour in a medium bowl and whisk to remove any lumps. Make a well in the center of the flour. While stirring with a fork, slowly pour in ½ cup (120 ml) plus 1 tablespoon (15 ml) of the heavy cream. Continue to stir until the dough has mostly come together. With your hands, gather the dough, incorporating any dry flour, and form into a ball.

2. Place the dough on a lightly floured board and pat into a rectangle that is ½ to ¾ inch (1.3 to 2 cm) thick. Fold in half. Turn and repeat. Pat the dough into a ¾-inch-thick (2 cm) square. Cut dough into 4 equally sized square biscuits.

3. Preheat the air fryer at 325°F (170°C) for 3 minutes. Spray the air fryer basket with oil to prevent sticking. Place the biscuits in the air fryer basket. Cook for 15 to 18 minutes until the tops are browned and the insides fully cooked. (May be done ahead.)

4. To make the peaches, cut the peaches in half and remove the pit. Brush the peach halves with the melted butter and sprinkle ½ teaspoon of the brown sugar and ¼ teaspoon of the cinnamon on each peach half. Arrange the peaches in a single layer in the air fryer basket. Cook at 375°F (190°C) for 8 to 10 minutes until the peaches are soft and the tops caramelized.

SHORTCAKES

1 cup (125 g) self-rising flour

½ cup (120 ml) plus 1 tablespoon (15 ml) heavy cream

Vegetable oil for spraying

CARAMELIZED PEACHES

2 peaches, preferably freestone

1 tablespoon (14 g) unsalted butter, melted

2 teaspoons brown sugar

1 teaspoon cinnamon

WHIPPED CREAM

1 cup (235 ml) cold heavy cream

1 tablespoon (13 g) granulated sugar

½ teaspoon vanilla extract

Zest of 1 lime

5. While the peaches are cooking, whip the cream. Pour the cold heavy cream, sugar, and vanilla (if using) into the bowl of a stand mixer or a metal mixing bowl. Beat with the whisk attachment for your stand mixer or a handheld electric mixer on high speed until stiff peaks form, about 1 minute. (If not using the cream right away, cover with plastic wrap and refrigerate until needed.)

6. To assemble the shortcakes, cut each biscuit in half horizontally. Place a peach on the bottom half of each biscuit and place the top half on top of the peach. Top each shortcake with whipped cream and a sprinkle of lime zest. Serve immediately.

INDEX

ALSO AVAILABLE

Rice Cooker
978-0-7603-9741-1

Grilling
978-0-7603-9747-3

Smoking
978-0-7603-9745-9